KATHRYN AT HOME

KATHRYN AT HOME

A GUIDE TO SIMPLE ENTERTAINING

Kathryn M. Ireland

with Ithaka Roddam

GIBBS SMITH
TO ENRICH AND INSPIRE HUMANKIND

To Tarka, Tatiana, Tilly,
Sidonie, and Lola —
the daughters I didn't
give birth to

20 19 18 17 16   5 4 3 2 1

Text © 2016 by Kathryn M. Ireland
Illustrations © 2016 by Lucilla Caine
Photograph credits on page 223

Published by
Gibbs Smith
P.O. Box 667
Layton, Utah 84041

1.800.835.4993 orders
www.gibbs-smith.com

Designed by Doug Turshen with David Huang

Gibbs Smith books are printed on paper produced from
sustainable PEFC-certified forest/controlled wood source.
Learn more at www.pefc.org.
Printed and bound in Hong Kong

ISBN: 978-1-4236-4071-4

Library of Congress Control Number: 2015959079

Contents

Foreword
by Kate Betts

The first time I saw photos of Kathryn's bohemian-chic French farmhouse, La Castellane, I knew I wanted to sit at her table. What's more, I wanted to set my table just like her table. I wanted to learn all of Kathryn's entertaining secrets — from the colorful Moroccan linens to the terra-cotta pots of lavender and the way she pulls together a seemingly spontaneous guest list and then effortlessly creates a magical evening or afternoon. Who can resist her gorgeous table settings, simple yet so chic and inviting with tiny vases of fresh garden roses and brass candelabras dripping with wax?

Kathryn is the ultimate connoisseur: she knows the right wine to serve, the recipe for pot de crème, or the outdoor market where they sell the tartest apple cider. She's also something of a set designer, whether she is creating pink candlelight at dusk, early morning breakfasts by a lavender-scented fire, or a pile of paisley pillows under a shady oak tree for an afternoon nap al fresco. More than Kathryn's tables or her scrumptious food and inimitable settings, it's the glow on her guests' faces inviting us into the photo.

"I'll have a dinner for you" is a familiar refrain for anyone who has been so lucky to call her a friend. And with Kathryn, the genius of her invitation — whether it be to an 18th-century barn overlooking Provençal fields or a Eucalyptus-filled garden in Venice — is that she takes such pleasure in setting her table and gathering familiar and new friends around a feast. In fact, it's hard to imagine someone with a bigger heart or a better sense of style when it comes to entertaining.

Preface
by Ithaka Roddam

When I think of my childhood summers, almost every one was spent at Kathryn's houses either in France or LA.

I was one of four girls, and Kathryn had three sons of similar ages. With the boys' friends and cousins, there were always about ten of us kids running around. Each of us was assigned a chore every day throughout the summer holidays, things like setting the table, feeding the horses, or watering the garden. Picking the vegetables from the kitchen garden was one of my favorite jobs. I used to walk barefoot in the prickly grass with my mum and Kathryn, carrying a straw basket and a pair of sécateurs (pruning snips). They would show me which herbs to pick and what was ripe, and we would fill the baskets with the freshest lettuce leaves, tomatoes warm from the sun, sweet strawberries, and roses to adorn the tables. Another chore was lighting the hundreds of tea lights in the wall nooks of the barn, which was pretty tedious but certainly kept us busy for a while! I realized from a young age what a difference candlelight made to the romantic ambiance of the barn for dinner.

Kathryn has an amazing ability to create something out of nothing. The entertaining space that she inhabits has to look beautiful. I remember moving a table from one oak tree to another three or four times until it was in the right place. It is little details like this, which Kathryn has an eye for, that make the party flow. When I think of Kathryn's dinners and parties over the years, there was always Elvis playing, delicious rosé on tap, some of the most interesting and fun people, and an element of surprise. You never knew how the night might begin or end.

My mum, Carina Cooper, wrote cookbooks and my father, Franc, created the television program "MasterChef," so I have always grown up with the idea that mealtime was a celebration and was inspired to cook on my own from a very early age. I often helped Mum cook big lunches for all the guests at Kathryn's homes. I think I was about twelve years old when I first began making up recipes of my own and was always delighted by their success! In my early twenties Kathryn asked me at the last minute to cook for her first design/yoga retreat. It became the detox/retox week, and one of my most memorable summers. I cooked and cooked and it really was the beginning of a new culinary chapter in my life.

Since then, whenever I can, I help Kathryn at her retreats or special dinners in LA, and now I have been given the privilege of cooking, styling, and photographing for this book. I was truly inspired by the farmers markets in and around Santa Monica and am really taken with the Californian lifestyle and the outdoor living that Kathryn creates.

The recipes in this book are inspired by long summer lunches with a farm-to-table style in mind, using fresh and local ingredients.

Introduction
by Kathryn M. Ireland

Entertaining is my passion and it comes naturally to me. As with producing anything, you can't rely on just one element. It's the combination of delicious food, above-average wines, amazing decor, and, most importantly, people who have something to say — a unique mix, effortlessness that makes the guests feel comfortable, people you wouldn't normally put together, wonderful chaos, as my great friend the film director Jaci Judelson would say, that allows for spontaneity.

It takes courage and a leap of faith to entertain in one's home. Mishaps are expected and part of the charm of doing the party yourself; some great things often come out of mistakes. Who wants a perfectly boring dinner, house, or anything? There has to be the element of the unexpected for the experience to be real.

This book came about in a very organic way. Having bought a house in the French countryside a quarter of a century ago, which went from two bedrooms to twelve over the years, I was able to teach myself how to cook, clean, and make beds! It has been home to not only my children and me but also my best friends and their children. Ithaka was born within months of my eldest son, Oscar, and was amongst the first of our guests when she was an infant. Over the years, we have cooked together with her mother, Carina Cooper, a noted chef and author of numerous cookbooks, whose style and tastes have evolved over the years. In the kitchen there is always a combination of tradition and different influences, from California, Guatemala, Mexico, India, Sri Lanka, Italy, and of course, France.

What interests me the most is entertaining for groups (that's

what I know). How to bring farm to table on a daily basis starts
with the produce that you either grow yourself or buy locally.
I've watched Ithaka, from a young child to now, develop her love
of food and knowledge of what goes with what.

Something I learned on my own was how to cook for many — groups
of sixteen and more, where having a budget and a time frame for
the organizing and prep work are essential to the success of the
meal. Many of my early recipes when I was doing all the cooking
were for quiches and tarts, both savory and sweet, using ready-
made pastry shells, and I could produce pizzas in record time.
The children were little and there were many of them, so that
was where I excelled. As the years went by, the kitchen became
where we all hung out, whether it was a group venture or a place
to stay cool in the summer. The prep kitchen now is where the
old wine cellar was. Ithaka has calmly cooked in the wine cellar
since childhood; she has scoured the markets with us all, walked
the country lanes picking wild fruits and berries, and produced
mouthwatering dishes from an early age. The laughter, dancing, and
creativity that came from that room never ceased to amaze me.

Watching all of these children grow up has been my raison
d'être for working with Ithaka on this book, and it has been an
honor. Most of the recipes are Ithaka's; a few are from friends.

I am constantly having to teach restraint, and I always liken
decorating to food: one too many ingredients can throw the whole
taste off.

This book is really a scrapbook of recipes, tabletop decor,
notes from various journals that I've kept over the years, wines
that I have loved. There really is so much to think about when
entertaining, from the color of the candles to the appropriate
background music. It's much more than what we shall eat, although
that is the number-one priority. It gives me such pleasure to
invite friends and friends of friends to my home, and even more
pleasure to see people enjoy themselves. This book is dedicated
to all of you who have been at my table.

Enjoy!

Rise and
Shine

One of the luxuries of life is breakfast.
Not just grabbing a cup of coffee and an
egg sandwich to eat in the car on the way
to work, but taking time to make a meal. I'm not someone
who jumps out of bed ravenous and wanting to eat immediately.
I love just being able to hang around in my nightie without
any sense of urgency. Going from lemon water to cappuccino to
fresh-squeezed orange juice, taking time to read the papers
and gossip with best friends — this is the best kind of Sunday
morning. Eating a croissant with delicious homemade jam and
boiling an egg is a genteel way to start the day. For most of
us, this kind of breakfast happens on weekends and holidays.
There's something to be said for the luxury of time. It's
something that's hard to find. We work long hours; there is no
longer standard business days — 9 to 5 is now 7 to 10.

When my boys were little, breakfast was a big deal. A
ritual. I would lay the table the night before. It was always a
rush to get them dressed, fed, out the door, and off to school
with lunches in hand. Eggy bread or breakfast quesadillas were
their favorites. As they got older and could open the lid of
the Aga, they loved to fry eggs directly on the cooktop.

To me, the decor and look of the table are as important
as the food. I love throwing a cloth on the table and taking
a few minutes to lay it, even if it's picnic style. In the
kitchen especially, I find that a lot of people overthink what
goes where. Yes, it is a talent knowing where to put things;
but as with anything, the more you do something, the better
you get. It all becomes seamless. Table settings and cooking
belong together.

Breakfast like a king,
lunch like a prince,
dine like a pauper.

—Anonymous

Honey and Lemon Morning Kick-Starter

This is a really healthy morning pick-me-up, especially if you are feeling under the weather. It has a real kick to it. I like to drink this and have a bowl of California Bircher Muesli (page 28) for a good, nourishing breakfast. —Ithaka

MAKES A TEAPOT

Juice and rind of 1 lemon
2 tablespoons organic or local honey
1 teaspoon Chinese five-spice powder
A sprinkling of cayenne pepper
1 sprig rosemary
3 slices fresh gingerroot
A pot of boiling water

In your teapot, add the lemon juice and rind and the honey; stir and mix well. Add the spice, pepper, rosemary, and ginger, and finely top with boiling water, again giving it a good stir. Let brew for a few minutes before serving.

WAKE UP AND STRETCH

Side stretch
Up dog, down dog
Calf stretch
Triangle pose
Mountain pose
Warrior 1
Warrior 2
Triangle pose
Child pose
Beloved pigeon pose

California Bircher Muesli

This is such a feel-good breakfast, you can literally taste the goodness! It's super easy. The only thing to note is that you have to make it the night before so that the oats really soak up the liquid and become soft. There are no rules to this recipe; you can add as many fruits, nuts, or seeds as you please — mix and match. Below is one of my favorite combos.
—Ithaka

SERVES 2

  1 cup (200 g) rolled oats
  3/4 cup (170 g) organic natural live
     yogurt
  1 Gala apple, grated with skin on
  1 tablespoon water
  1 teaspoon cinnamon, divided
  1 dessertspoon maple syrup, honey, or
     agave
  2 tablespoons shredded coconut
  1 tablespoon chopped raw pistachio
     nuts
  1 tablespoon chopped hazelnuts
  1 tablespoon pumpkin seeds
  Chia seeds and flax seeds, optional
  1 handful of raspberries
  1 handful of blueberries

In a mixing bowl, add the oats, three-fourths of the yogurt, half the grated apple, a tablespoon of water, a pinch of the cinnamon, and the syrup; mix well. Cover and refrigerate overnight.

In the morning, toast the coconut and nuts in a frying pan for a couple of minutes with the rest of the cinnamon, until golden. Take the oat mixture out of the fridge and mix in three-fourths of the nuts and the rest of the grated apple.

Serve in a glass or bowl of your choice by layering the berries at the bottom. Spoon in the oats, then a layer of yogurt, another spoon of oats, and finish off with the rest of the berries and a sprinkling of nuts.

Hard-Boiled Eggs

Everyone boils an egg about the
same way, but the results can
vary. Here is how I do it:

• Put eggs in a saucepan large
enough to hold them in a single
layer. Then add cold water to
cover the eggs by 1 inch. Heat
over high heat just to boiling.

• Remove pan from the heat.
Either serve in an egg cup, or
if removing the shell, do so by
cracking the egg on the side
of the saucepan and remove the
shell under cold water. —Kathryn

Perfect Poached Eggs

Properly poached eggs are one of
life's simple pleasures and not
so hard to get right. I always
use free-range eggs and Maldon
sea salt in the water. Poached
eggs can be eaten simply on a
piece of toasted bread with a
dash of salt and pepper or over
a salad and vegetables. —Kathryn

• Make sure the eggs are really
fresh.

• Add a small dash of vinegar to
a pan of simmering water.

• Crack the eggs individually
into a ramekin or cup.

• Create a whirlpool in the
water to help the egg white wrap
around the yolk.

• Slowly tip the egg into the
water, white first. Cook for 3
minutes.

• Remove carefully with a
slotted spoon.

Green Eggs and . . .

Poached eggs on sourdough with avocado, basil pesto, green chili, and heirloom cherry tomatoes. This is my version of avocado on toast: it's got the eggs, it's got the avo, and it's got a little bit extra. —Ithaka

SERVES 2

Sea salt
White wine vinegar
2 large organic eggs
1 avocado
4 heirloom cherry tomatoes
1 green medium-heat chili pepper
2 slices white or brown sourdough bread
Fresh Homemade Basil Pesto (page 36)
Extra virgin olive oil
Freshly ground black pepper
2 leaves of fresh basil
Juice of 1 lime

Bring a large shallow pan of water to the boil with a pinch of sea salt and a dash of white wine vinegar. Give the water a stir, so a little current is created, then one by one gently crack in the 2 eggs and let simmer for 5 minutes, or more if you prefer harder eggs.

Meanwhile, thinly slice the avocado into half-moons, quarter the tomatoes, and finely chop a little bit of the chili pepper (depending on how much heat you can handle). Slice 2 pieces of bread and lightly toast. When the eggs are ready, gently ladle them out with a slotted spoon and set aside to let the water run off.

Spread a dollop of pesto evenly onto the toasts, add a layer of avocado and the tomatoes, season with a drizzle of olive oil, salt, pepper, some torn basil leaves, chopped chili pepper, and a squeeze of lime juice. Carefully place the eggs on the toast and top with some extra pesto and seasoning. Serve with a large pot of coffee.

Fresh Homemade Basil Pesto

My version is inspired by a combination of the pesto recipes of my mother, Carina Cooper, and Kathryn's L.A. chef, Jaqueline Dessoubre. Use for breakfast in the morning or on pasta for dinner. —Ithaka

1 large bunch fresh garden basil
1 garlic clove
1/4 cup good-quality extra virgin olive oil
1 cup (200 g) good-quality fresh Parmesan cheese
Sea salt
Freshly ground black pepper

Wash the basil and place in a blender, food processor, or deep bowl if you are using a hand blender. Crush in the garlic and add 3 to 4 tablespoons olive oil; blend until it is the consistency of pesto.

Add the grated Parmesan and season with salt and pepper; blend again. The more Parmesan you add, the thicker it will get. Taste it and adjust the cheese and oil to your liking. Use immediately on bruschetta or pasta. Or spoon it into a jar and keep in the refrigerator for later; it will last 3 to 5 days in the fridge. Adding a film of oil over the top will help hold the bright color.

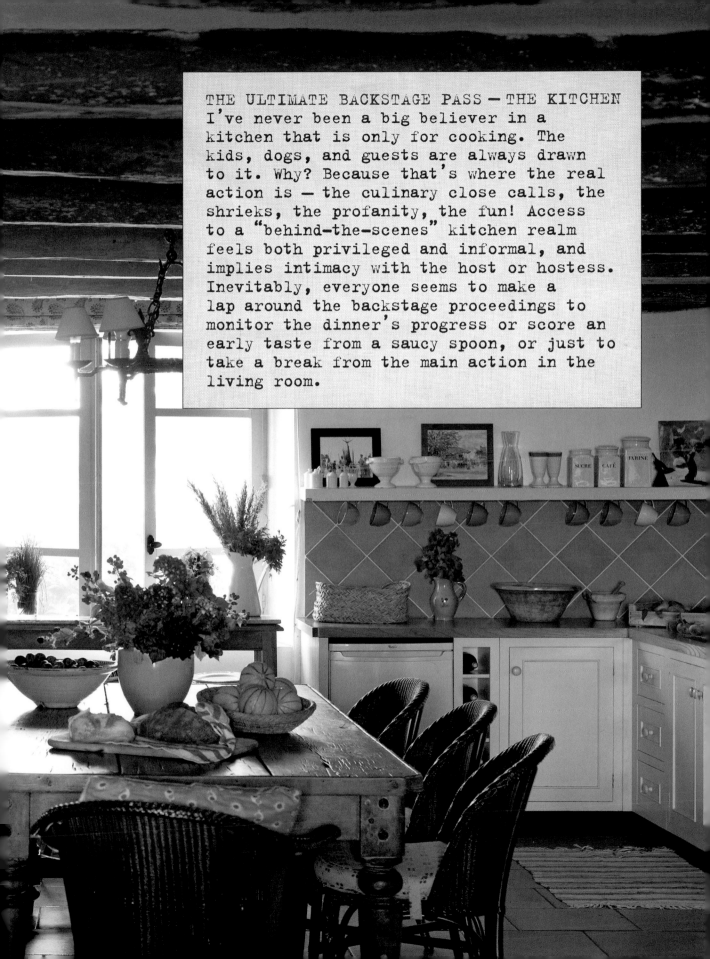

THE ULTIMATE BACKSTAGE PASS — THE KITCHEN

I've never been a big believer in a kitchen that is only for cooking. The kids, dogs, and guests are always drawn to it. Why? Because that's where the real action is — the culinary close calls, the shrieks, the profanity, the fun! Access to a "behind-the-scenes" kitchen realm feels both privileged and informal, and implies intimacy with the host or hostess. Inevitably, everyone seems to make a lap around the backstage proceedings to monitor the dinner's progress or score an early taste from a saucy spoon, or just to take a break from the main action in the living room.

Kitchen Essentials

- Spiralizer
- Colander
- Chopping board
- Set of good knives
- Peelers
- Blender
- Bread bin
- Casserole pot
- Salad bowls (different sizes)
- Large platters (various sizes; white)
- Pyrex dishes, oven to table
- Oven gloves
- Tea towels
- Corkscrew
- Ice
- Cocktail shaker
- Tumblers
- Lots of glasses
- Serving spoons
- Aprons
- Cheese grater
- Pots, large and small, for pasta and sauces
- Glass jars
- Matches

Ithaka's Kitchen Rules & Cooking Tips

There are a few important rules and rituals I follow when buying food and entering the kitchen. They are not difficult and by no means a chore — just a few thoughts that make a difference in my culinary experience. I hope they do yours, too.

1 No matter how good or bad or experienced you are in the kitchen, you should never cook if you are in a bad mood. When cooking, you are creating something from within. Your emotions, mind, and energy go into creating a beautiful, delicious meal, and, believe me, your friends and family will taste the goodness if that is the intention you put into making your food.

2 This is easier said than done, but if you are able to buy fresh, organic produce, it is worth the extra effort, as you will taste and feel the difference. Buy fruit and vegetables that are in season and local to your area if possible. Use and support your local farmers markets and independent stores.

3 ALWAYS wash your fruit and veg, even if the package says already washed in spring water.

4 Butter is not bad for you; it's a good fat that makes food taste delicious. Use extra virgin olive oil, not light. Never use fat free dairy or packaged food. Natural fat is essential to your daily diet and health.

5 Use gray rock salt for cooking and sea salt flakes, like Maldon, for the table. You get all the minerals from the gray rock salt that we are missing in everyday life.

Always use freshly ground black pepper and freshly squeezed lemon juice, none of that bottled stuff.

6 Using fresh herbs is something that I learned from my mum; she always just threw a handful of fresh herbs on top of everything and it always made the food taste fresh and more interesting than without herbs. Growing your own is not hard; whether in a kitchen garden or even in windowsill containers, you can have an abundance of fresh herbs at your fingertips. The five top herbs to plant and use regularly:

Basil
Rosemary
Mint
Chives
Parsley

Sage, thyme, cilantro, and dill are also worth planting or buying fresh at the market. I rarely use dried herbs.

7 NEVER cook in a dirty kitchen. You should always start the prep with clean work surfaces and an empty, spotless sink. If you can wash up along the way, it just makes life easier.

8 Cooking is fun — it shouldn't be a chore. Creating something from scratch and turning your ingredients into a delicious meal is truly a joy, a whole process, and the more people you share it with, the better.

Homemade Raspberry and Vanilla Bean Jam

If you have time to make your own
jams and preserves in the summer,
there is nothing more satisfying.
—Ithaka

MAKES 3–4 JARS

   2 pounds (1 k) raspberries
   Juice of 1/2 lemon
   2 1/2 cups (500 g) superfine sugar
      (golden caster sugar or pectin sugar)
   1 vanilla bean, split lengthwise

Before you begin, wash and sterilize your
jam jars according to standard canning
practices.

For the jam, stir half the raspberries, the
lemon juice, and the sugar together in a
large pan and let simmer on a low heat for
5 to 7 minutes.

Add the vanilla pod and the rest of the
berries and gently boil for another 5 to 7
minutes. Remove any foam along the way.

Remove the pod, scraping any remaining
seeds and paste into the mixture. Let rest
for 15 minutes before ladling it into the
jam jars and applying lids.

Jam can be stored in the fridge or pantry
for 6 to 8 weeks. Enjoy it with a baguette
or add a dollop in your hot cereal.

NOTE: DO NOT ADD COLD JAM TO HOT JARS, OR HOT
JAM TO COLD JARS; THE JARS COULD SHATTER.

Breakfast Banana Loaf

You can't go wrong with a treat like warm banana bread just out of the oven for breakfast with a pot of coffee or some hot chocolate. It's so comforting and something different to add to the morning spread. —Ithaka

MAKES 1 LOAF

- 3/4 cup (175 g) soft brown sugar
- 2 sticks (200 g) unsalted butter, softened
- 2 free-range organic eggs
- 1 cup (200 g) self-rising flour
- 1 teaspoon cinnamon
- 1 teaspoon nutmeg
- 4 ripe bananas, mashed

Preheat the oven to 350°F (180°C).

In a mixing bowl, cream together the sugar, butter, and eggs. Gradually add the flour and spices and whisk well. Add the mashed banana at the end, making sure the cake batter is well blended and has a creamy, smooth texture.

Lightly grease a loaf pan with some butter and a sprinkling of flour; this really helps with taking the banana bread out of the pan. Spoon the mixture into the pan and even it out. Bake for 30 to 45 minutes, or until firm and golden. Test with a skewer inserted into the middle of the cake; if it comes out clean, it is ready. Let cool for 10 minutes before removing from the pan. Serve warm.

Blueberry Banana Pancakes

Pancakes with fresh fruit makes a filling, high-energy breakfast. Use whatever fruits you like; this is a favorite combo of my guests. — Kathryn

SERVES 2

    1 1/2 ripe bananas, divided
    2/3 cup almond milk, more if needed
    3/4 cup flour of your choice (I like
        wheat or oat)
    1 teaspoon baking powder
    1/4 teaspoon cinnamon (optional)
    2 dashes of salt
    1/2 cup blueberries, divided
    4 teaspoons coconut or vegetable oil,
        for the pan, divided
    Maple syrup, heated, for serving

Using a hand-held blender, mix 1 banana with the almond milk until well blended.

In a separate bowl, mix the flour, baking powder, cinnamon, and salt together. Pour the milk mixture into the flour mixture and stir until just combined. (If the batter is too thick, add a bit more milk.) Reserve 2 heaping tablespoons of blueberries and stir the rest into the batter.

Heat 2 teaspoons of oil in a large nonstick skillet over medium heat. Pour 1/4 cup of the pancake batter into the pan. Watch for bubbles to form in the batter, then flip the pancake. Cook the other side for about a minute. Be sure the pancake is cooked all the way through; if not, reduce the heat and let it cook a bit longer. Repeat for the second pancake, or until the batter is gone.

Slice the remaining 1/2 banana and divide it, along with the reserved blueberries, over the two servings. Pour maple syrup over the top.

Markets are addictive. One of my greatest pleasures in life is the open air market in Gaillac, an old medieval town an hour's drive from my home in France. Because I only go once a week, I've learned to do all my errands on foot in the maze of traffic-free streets before I shop the vibrant farmers' stalls for the colorful mounds of seasonal fresh produce.

After all these years, I've finally trained myself to let supply determine my demand — and the menu! The market inspires me to experiment with vegetables and fruits not readily available at my Santa Monica farmers market, such as Italian bergamots, sorrel, black radishes, mâche, and fresh prunes (yes, they exist).

What's in Season

The only way to decide on daily menus is to know
what's in season and to shop local. Don't even think of
exotic, out-of-season fruits that need to be flown in,
or fruits and vegetables that are force-grown, picked
early so as to ripen on the long trip to market.

FRANCE, JUNE/JULY

- Asparagus
- Courgettes
- Artichokes
- Lettuces
- Apricots
- Blackcurrants
- Redcurrants
- Radishes
- Peas
- Carrots
- Melons
- Rhubarb
- Beets

AUGUST/SEPTEMBER

- Blackberries
- Figs
- Cherry tomatoes
- Peaches
- Plums
- Pears
- Grapes
- Potatoes
- Broccoli

CALIFORNIA, OCTOBER/NOVEMBER

- Avocados
- Apples
- Basil
- Brussels sprouts
- Cabbage
- Carrots
- Chard
- Cauliflower
- Figs
- Grapefruits
- Lemons
- Tangerines
- Corn
- Cucumbers
- Eggplants
- Kale
- Mushrooms
- Pomegranates
- Squash
- Tomatoes

DECEMBER

- Chestnuts
- Mustard
- Chili
- Turnips
- Yams
- Potatoes
- Peppers
- Spinach

CALIFORNIA GROWN

Fashionably Floral

As someone who freely
embraces sensory overload,
I positively vibrate in
the presence of a market
stall of fresh flowers.
Typically, I allow
the natural cycle to
determine my flower menu
and stick to the gorgeous
blooms in season: lilacs
and peonies in spring;
fragrant English roses in
June; sunflowers in August;
and jewel-tone mums in
the autumn months — one
beautiful act following
the next. With armfuls
of budding branches and
stems in full bloom, you
can create a lush garden
anywhere. Feel free to
dazzle with seasonal
blossoms and don't be
afraid to go to extremes.

Design Retreats

The design retreats, aka Detox/Retox, came out of my newfound love of teaching and entertaining. For many years, I've hosted hundreds — probably thousands — of people in France and realized that it was breaking the bank. There had to be a way to cover my expenses. Having people stay is more than just having a bed and clean sheets. Delicious foods, wines, activities, the other guests that come to mingle all play a large part in creating memories. With my twenty plus years of knowledge in interior design, I realized that I had much invaluable knowledge and resources that I would be happy to share with my guests.

Design enthusiasts worldwide have been coming to La Castellane for the last five years. The week-long retreats have been so successful that now we offer Design Boot Camps in Los Angeles, as three-day intensive course for those working on a project. Some are designers; others want to consult with design experts without having to commit to an interior designer. This has become a whole other chapter for me.

A visit to La Castellane is to enter into the stylish world of Kathryn Ireland. A fabulous trip filled with relaxation, style, great food, adventure, and laughter. We dined and lunched around her home enjoying the lovely French countryside, table set with gorgeous linens, rosé, all done with a chic casual feel that instantly makes you feel warm and welcome. Daily outings to magical medieval towns, where we would find local delicacies from quaint open markets that were then exquisitely prepared for us. Design chats by the pool or by a cozy fire, so inspirational to me to slow down amongst my peers. The best part is I have made lifelong friends through the process. My first visit was such a fabulous time that I had to return the following year. How could I not, with Kathryn as the hostess?

—Kathy Marshall

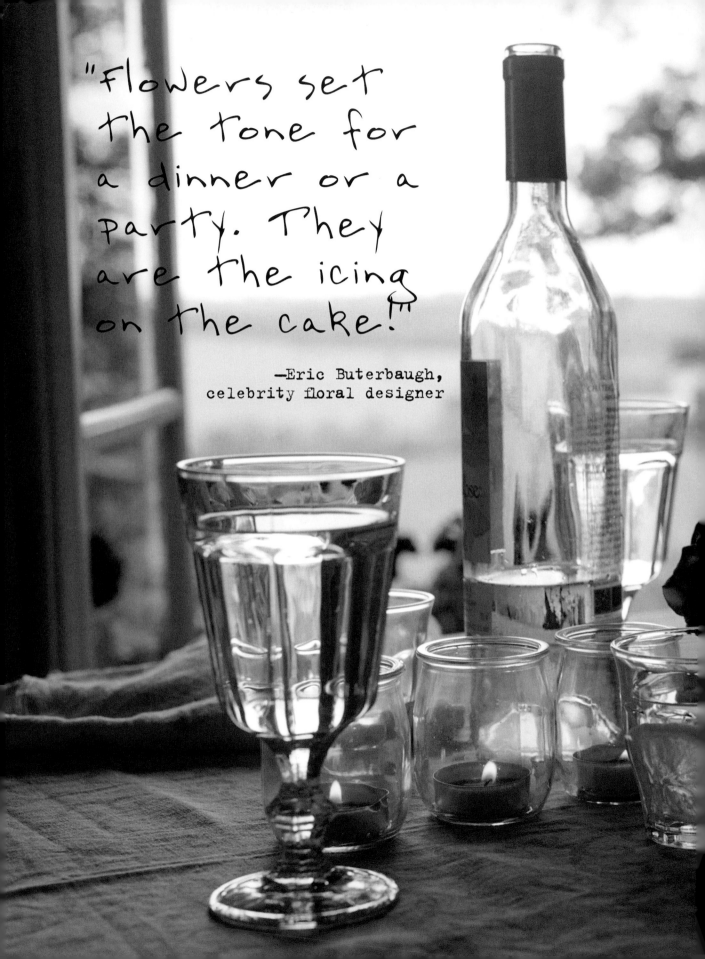

"Flowers set the tone for a dinner or a party. They are the icing on the cake!"

—Eric Buterbaugh,
celebrity floral designer

Finders Keepers

Even though shopping is as close as the nearest laptop, my approach veers sharply from the keyboard-clicking route. I still love to treasure hunt in the field. That's why, no matter where I am, I hit the local flea markets for overlooked relics and artisanal crafts. As someone who favors colorful and eclectic tablescapes, I can never have too many vintage plates, linens, glassware, flatware, or breadboards. Every now and then, I'll even stumble into a stroke of dumb luck. One of my great scores was a full intact set of Limoges plates! They'd been a wedding present, and who knows why they'd never been used. It's worth it to do the legwork.

Larder Essentials

OILS AND VINEGARS

- Extra virgin olive oil
- Sunflower oil
- Rapeseed oil
- Coconut oil
- Sesame oil
- Unsalted butter
- Balsamic vinegar
- Apple cider vinegar
- White wine vinegar

GRAINS

- Quinoa
- Puy lentils
- Arborio rice
- Basmati rice
- Porridge oats
- Polenta

PASTAS

- Spaghetti
- Penne
- Fusilli

CANS

- Tomatoes
- Borlotti (cranberry) beans
- Black olives
- Capers
- Anchovies
- Tuna

JARS AND BOTTLES

- Grainy mustard
- Dijon mustard
- Lea and Perrins worchestershire sauce
- Soy sauce
- Tabasco
- Chutney
- Honey
- Jam
- Marmalade
- Maple syrup
- Coffee
- Tea

BAKING

- Plain flour
- Self-rising flour
- Baking powder
- Baking soda
- Fine granulated sugar (golden caster)
- Light brown sugar
- Vanilla extract

SPICES

- Cumin
- Cinnamon
- Nutmeg
- Turmeric
- Cayenne pepper
- Paprika
- Black peppercorns
- Rock salt
- Maldon sea salt
- Stock (vegetable Bouillon)

Larder Essentials

Heirloom Cherry Tomato and Calendula Flower Salsa

At the Santa Monica Farmers Market on a Wednesday or Saturday morning, it is more than likely that there will be a few stalls selling fresh calendula flowers, and more than enough for this tomato dish. I have also found them at Whole Foods. Or you may be lucky enough to grow them in your own garden. —Ithaka

2 punnets of mixed colored heirloom cherry tomatoes
2 garlic cloves, crushed
1 small bunch fresh cilantro
1 medium-hot red chili, finely chopped
Extra virgin olive oil
Sea salt
Freshly ground black pepper
1 lime
1 box calendula flowers

Wash and quarter the tomatoes and place in a mixing bowl. Add the crushed garlic, some roughly chopped cilantro and half a finely chopped red chili; season with a dash of olive oil, salt, pepper, and a squeeze of lime.

Gently wash and remove a few petals from the calendula flowers; add the petals to the mix, leaving some whole for decoration. Taste and season again if necessary.

This zingy salsa goes especially well with warm cornbread.

Lunch Under the Oak Tree

Summer picnics in the sunshine with friends and family always evoke lunch, with an array of salads, summer soups, fresh breads, berries, and homemade sorbets.

My self-taught cooking abilities are not bad. There are certain things I have figured out, mastered, and love to cook. The rest, I leave to others. I am very opinionated when it comes to food. Living between two continents that both excel in the food department, I am lucky enough to be surrounded by not only great produce but restaurants and chefs that are innovative and whose simplicity is refreshing.

One of my oldest school friends, ZaZa Guirey, taught me to always have a simple pesto available year-round. Just basil, garlic, and olive oil. As you get to the bottom of the bottle, replenish it. Jaqueline Dessoubre, my chef of many years in Santa Monica, always made sure that we had homemade tomato sauce in the fridge. With some of these simple ingredients on hand, I was able to throw together lunch for sixteen to twenty at the drop of a hat!

A picnic says "informal." It's my favorite word that expresses we are eating casually, either indoors or outdoors. It lets your guests know there will be no placement and no silver!

tortillas

cheese straws

figs

enchilladas

salsa

nuts

beetroot

houmous

tomatoes

courgette

halloumi

Braised Baby Artichokes with Lemon

I would serve this on its own or
with a small board of assorted
goat cheeses. It's so simple,
and yet it really should be the
center of the meal. —Ithaka

SERVES 2

6 baby artichokes
Extra virgin olive oil
Sea salt
Freshly ground black pepper
Juice of 1 lemon

Bring a large pot of salted water to the boil
and add the artichokes; cook for 10 to 12
minutes. When soft, drain and slice down
the middle.

Heat a drizzle of olive oil in a large frying
pan over medium heat; fry the artichokes
for 5 to 7 minutes, until golden. Sprinkle
with the lemon juice. Season with salt
and pepper. Remove from the heat and
serve hot.

A Light Green Cod Salad

This is so fresh, so healthy, and absolutely delicious. It's perfect for a light lunch or early supper. I would even serve it as a starter before a main. —Ithaka

SERVES 2

2 cod fillets
2 garlic cloves, crushed
3 tablespoons (50 g) butter, chopped into cubes
Extra virgin olive oil
Sea salt
4 ounces (1 box) lamb's lettuce (aka corn salad or mâche), washed
2 endives, washed and cut into small half-circles
1 avocado, diced
1 cucumber

DRESSING:

2 tablespoons extra virgin olive oil
1 tablespoon maple syrup
Juice and zest of 1 lime
Juice of 1/2 lemon
2 tablespoons grated fresh ginger
Sea salt
Freshly ground black pepper

Preheat the oven to 350°F (180°C).

Place the cod on a sheet of tin foil with the crushed garlic, butter, a drizzle of olive oil, and a pinch of salt. Fold up the edges and tuck them in so that the fish is wrapped up like a parcel. Place on a baking tray in the oven and let steam for 10 to 12 minutes. The cooked fish should be soft and flaky. Remove fish from the foil and break it into flakes with a fork; let cool.

Place the lettuce into a nice salad bowl along with the endive and avocado. With a vegetable peeler, thinly slice the flesh from the cucumber lengthwise, stopping when you get to the seeds. Add the slices to the bowl.

For the dressing: Mix together the oil, syrup, juices, zest, and ginger. Add salt and pepper to taste; mix well.

Add the cooled fish to the salad along with the dressing. Season again if desired and serve immediately.

BEFORE THE BOWL: FRESH GREENS

Salad begins with the freshest greens. Smaller leaves can be kept whole, but tear the larger leaves, rather than chop, to minimize bruising. To wash the greens, swish them in a large bowlful or clean sink of cold water. To dry, use a spinner, or lift the greens from the water and spread them out on a clean tea towel. Pat dry and then roll up. Store the lettuce in the towel inside a clean plastic bag and chill until ready to use.

Cantaloupe with Parma Ham, Olive Oil, and Black Pepper

This is so easy and simple yet so fresh and delicious. It's perfect to go with a light lunch at La Castellane, Kathryn's summer home in the French countryside.
—Mia Lillingston

SERVES 8

2 ripe French cantaloupes
8 slices Parma ham
Best-quality extra virgin olive oil
Sea salt
Freshly ground black pepper

Cut the melon in half lengthwise and scoop out the seeds. Then slice each half into 4 lengthwise half-moon pieces. Drape a slice of Parma ham over each slice and set on a long serving dish. Drizzle the olive oil over each slice, sprinkle with a pinch of salt, and grind on the pepper. Serve for lunch with other light salads, a cheese board, and a baguette.

Dining outdoors under a sprawling tree is a daily ritual at La Castellane and has its own particular charm. Sometimes in the summer it's too hot to do anything but sit, eat, and share chilled bottles of rosé. For the menu I gravitate to no-cook, no-sweat, group-friendly buffets – great bread, cheeses, Spanish ham, local foie gras, and sliced fruits. Perhaps gazpacho made from garden tomatoes blended with a liberal amount of my neighbor's homemade bay and pimento-infused olive oil. The spread starts out as appetizers but then evolves into lunch that lingers well into the afternoon.

Kathryn and I took off in late afternoon with the horses and her Jack Russells. Kathryn had some kind of saddlebag, just big enough for a bottle of rosé and some olives. We rode out across hazy lavender fields as the sun was sinking behind the hills to a sunflower-choked slope, where the Tarn Valley unfolded in a panoramic, almost fairy-tale view of bucolic perfection — soft green forests, purpling sky, and lights flickering in a small village. It was, needless to say, a highlight moment. Especially since Kathryn forgot the wine glasses. So we glugged it in the gorgeous twilight and somehow made it home in complete darkness. —Mel Bourdeaux

THE IMPORTANCE OF BEING LABELED

Whatever you use for containers to transport your picnic lunch, it's a good idea to label the contents. Then guests don't have to unwrap each package to figure out what you've got. As with everything, the attractiveness of the packaging and the labels reflects your style.

AN HOUR OF ONE'S OWN

"A little while alone in your room will prove more valuable than anything else that could ever be given you." —Rumi

Sometimes one wants to spend time away from the crowd, social media, and telecommunications. Lazing about with a good book for an hour is my favorite way to unwind and recharge. Solitude enhances my creativity and concentration, and allows me to take a break from being "on" and rest up for the next event. Every now and then, one needs to entertain oneself.

Whole Baked French Goat Cheese Soufflé with Vine Tomatoes

This simple soufflé-style dish goes with many different salads and mains. It's such a delicious accompaniment, you are always left scraping the pot for more.
—Carina Cooper

SERVES 4

2 soft and crumbly French goat cheeses
2 vines of cherry tomatoes
Extra virgin olive oil
Sea salt
Freshly ground black pepper

Preheat the oven to 350°F (180°C).

For best results, I like to make this in an ovenproof ceramic pot; otherwise a small deep baking dish works as well. Place the whole goat cheese in the pot with washed cherry tomatoes, drizzle with olive oil, and sprinkle with a small pinch of salt.

Place in the oven and cook for 15 minutes, or until the cheese has melted and is bubbling. The juice of the tomatoes mixed with the oil and cheese creates a delectable soufflé-like texture, and the flavors really come together. When you take it out of the oven, grind on some black pepper. Serve it for lunch with a big green garden lettuce salad, a fresh warm baguette, and a glass of our favorite blush, Petale de Rosé.

Summer Green Minestrone Soup
with Grilled Poilâne Toast

Poilâne, the most popular country sourdough bread in France, is an excellent accompaniment to this wholesome yet light soup. It goes particularly well with a creamy goat cheese selection for the toast. —Ithaka

SERVES 12

2 tablespoons extra virgin olive oil

1 stick (about 50 g) unsalted butter

1 teaspoon vegetable bouillon powder

1 small yellow onion, roughly chopped

1 garlic clove, crushed

2 large zucchini

14 ounces (400 g) baby spinach

1 1/2 liters boiling water

1 large bunch arugula (rocket)

1 small bunch mint, thick stems
   removed

10 ounces (300 g) frozen small peas

Zest of 1 lemon

3 tablespoons crème fraîche

Sea salt

Freshly ground black pepper

Heat the olive oil, butter, and bouillon in a large pot over low heat. Add the onion and garlic and let cook.

Meanwhile, cut the zucchini into rough half-circles; add them to the pot. When the zucchini is lightly cooked, add the spinach and boiling water; stir well. When the zucchini and spinach have softened, remove the pot from the heat and set aside.

Add the arugula and mint to the pot, as well as the frozen peas and lemon zest. Whiz up the liquid mixture with an immersion blender until roughly smooth. Add the crème fraîche, and season to taste with salt and pepper. Return the blended soup to the stove and heat until hot but not boiling.

Serve with grilled sourdough toast. It is extra tasty with a dollop of Fresh Homemade Basil Pesto, page 36.

Beetroot and Crème Fraîche Purée with New Potatoes and Chives

The focus here is the beetroot purée, which you should make the day before or the morning of, as it takes a little while. It's so delicious and can also be used for smoked salmon bruschettas, on new potatoes, or as a dip. I created this recipe after having too many leftover roasted beets. —Ithaka

SERVES 5

   5 precooked red beetroots
   Extra virgin olive oil
   Balsamic vinegar
   Sea salt
   2/3 pound (300 g) baby new potatoes
   2 tablespoons crème fraîche
   Juice of 1/2 lemon
   Freshly ground black pepper
   1/4 cup (50 g) unsalted butter
   Fresh chives, for garnish

Preheat the oven to 375°F (190°C).

Cut the beetroots into circles and place on a baking sheet with a drizzle of olive oil, a splash of balsamic, and a pinch of salt. Place in the oven and roast for 15 minutes. Although the beets are already cooked, roasting them as well infuses the flavors better.

Meanwhile, heat a large pot of water with a pinch of salt on high heat. When it starts simmering, add the new potatoes and boil for 15 minutes. (You can tell when a potato is ready by sticking a fork into to it; if it is soft and begins to break, it is cooked.) Drain potatoes and set aside.

Remove beets from the oven and place in a blender or a deep bowl if you're using an immersion blender, and start to blend. Add in the crème fraîche, more olive oil if needed, and the lemon juice. Taste and season with salt and pepper.

Place the potatoes back into the pot and add the butter and salt and pepper to taste; set over a low heat to melt the butter and lightly heat the potatoes. Then add 4 to 6 dollops of the beet purée and toss together. Transfer to a serving dish and sprinkle with chives, a fine drizzle of olive oil, and some more black pepper. You can add more beet purée if desired; otherwise cover the rest and store in the fridge.

Green Bean, Butter Bean, and Parsley Salad
with Crispy Prosciutto

This salad is really easy to make, and if you don't eat meat, you can substitute tuna for the prosciutto. Green beans are abundant in July and later summer months, so it's great to use them in a salad like this. —Ithaka

SERVES 6–8

1 pound (400 g) slender green beans
8 ounces (130 g) Italian prosciutto
2 cans butter beans
Large bunch flat-leaf parsley

DRESSING
Extra virgin olive oil
Juice of 1 lemon
1 tablespoon balsamic vinegar
1 garlic clove, crushed and minced
Sea salt
Freshly ground black pepper

Bring a large pan of water to the boil with a pinch of salt. While it's heating up, prep the green beans by washing, topping, and tailing them.

Place the beans into the boiling water. Cook about 4 to 5 minutes, until softened but still crunchy. Drain immediately and run cold water over them to keep their color and stop the cooking.

Heat a small frying pan to medium-high, and fry the prosciutto until golden and crispy. It will dramatically shrink in size and release some oil. Once ready, place it on some paper towels to soak up any excess oil.

Drain and rinse the butter beans and place in a big serving bowl. Cut the green beans in half and add them to the butter beans. Roughly chop the parsley and it add to the mixture as well.

For the dressing, drizzle a large splash of the olive oil in a small jar or bowl with the lemon juice and vinegar. Add the garlic, and salt and pepper to taste; mix well.

Tear up the prosciutto and mix it into the beans. To finish, pour the dressing over the dish, toss well, and serve.

Zucchini Pizza on Short Crust

Anyone who grows zucchini in their garden knows that you always need more recipes for using it. For this pizza, pick the zucchinis while they are young and tender, before the glossy skin starts to dull. With Ithaka's short crust, this pizza makes a deliciously light lunch. —Kathryn

MAKES 1 PIZZA

1 Savory Short Crust Pastry
2 cups homemade tomato sauce
4 small zucchini, thinly sliced
Coarse salt
Freshly ground black pepper
Parmesan cheese, grated; optional

Preheat the oven to 400°F (200°C).

Prepare the short crust pastry. Because this is a very buttery crust, it needs to be prepared as directed rather than rolled, or it will become very sticky. Blind bake the crust for 10 to 15 minutes, until it turns a little brown.

Remove from the oven and evenly spread with the tomato sauce. Layer the zucchini (you can add other vegetables). Sprinkle the entire pizza with salt and pepper and bake for about 15 to 20 minutes, or until the zucchini are cooked through and lightly browned. If using cheese, add it for the last 5 minutes of cooking. Serve hot.

SAVORY SHORT CRUST PASTRY

4 tablespoons (130 g) unsalted butter, cut into small pieces
2 1/2 cups (350 g) all-purpose flour (plus extra for dusting)
1 large pinch of salt
Zest of 1/2 lemon
2 organic egg yolks
2 tablespoons cold milk or water

NOTE: YOU COULD ADD A PINCH OF PAPRIKA OR PARMESAN TO YOUR DOUGH, DEPENDING ON YOUR CHOICE OF FILLING. —ITHAKA

In a large mixing bowl, cream together the butter, flour, and salt using both hands; rub together until the mixture resembles course bread crumbs. Do not overwork; it should be light and crumbly. Now add the lemon zest, egg yolks, and milk; gently knead together and roll dough into a ball. It's important not to overwork the pastry, as it can become stretchy and elastic. Try to be light and confident with the kneading, as too much heat from your hands will melt the butter. When the dough ball is formed, shape it into a fat sausage-type roll and dust with flour before wrapping in plastic wrap. Refrigerate and let rest for at least 1 hour.

Cut the chilled pastry into slices 1 cm thick. Gently press those down onto the pizza pan one at a time, repeating and joining the slices together like a jigsaw puzzle until the whole crust is formed. When you get to the edges of the pan, gently push the dough toward the center so the edge is slightly thicker. Blind bake until the crust browns a little.

Grilled Figs with Goat Cheese, Thyme, and Honey

This is a great dish to make in late August, when figs are in abundance and their pungent smell permeates the air. There is something so divine about picking fresh figs right off their tree and eating a few along the way. This is a great appetizer or an accompaniment to other salads and mains. —Ithaka

SERVES 6–12

> 12 ripe figs
> 1 container soft, crumbly goat cheese
> 2 teaspoons runny honey
> A few sprigs of fresh thyme
> Extra virgin olive oil
> Sea salt
> Freshly ground black pepper
> 4 ounces (1 box) lamb's lettuce (aka
>   corn salad or mâche), washed

Wash the figs and cut off the stem, if there is one, then cut across through the fig, stopping just before you get to the bottom. Place the figs on a baking tray and set aside.

In a bowl, mix together the goat cheese, honey, thyme leaves, and 1 teaspoon of oil. Season with salt and pepper. Stuff a small teaspoonful of the mixture into each fig. Drizzle them with olive oil and place under the broiler for 5 to 10 minutes, depending on how hot your oven is.

Meanwhile, scatter the lettuce over a large, flat serving plate. When the figs are ready and the cheese is melty and bubbling over, take them out of the oven and gently place over the salad. Serve immediately.

Couscous with Green Onions, Cilantro, and Toasted Pine Nuts

I first made this to go with a Toulouse sausage and red pepper dish, but it actually works well with a cumin butterflied lamb as well as chicken and zucchini brochettes. It's fresh and light yet stands well on its own.
—Ithaka

SERVES 6–8

1 pound (about 500 g) couscous
5–6 tablespoons (75 g) unsalted butter
Sea salt
Boiling water
6 green onions
Zest and juice of 1 lemon
1 big bunch fresh cilantro, roughly chopped
3/4 cup (100 g) pine nuts
Extra virgin olive oil
Sea salt
Freshly ground black pepper

Place the couscous in a large mixing bowl with the butter and a pinch of salt. Pour in enough boiling water to just cover the couscous, and then cover with a lid or large plate and let steep for 5 to 7 minutes. When all the water is absorbed, give it a good toss; it should become fluffy. Set aside.

Meanwhile finely chop the green onions into half-moons, grate the lemon zest, and roughly wash and chop the cilantro. Set aside separately.

Heat a small frying pan over medium-high heat; place the pine nuts in the pan and cook until they become golden brown; keep an eye out, as they burn quickly.

To the couscous, add a good drizzle of olive oil, a large pinch of salt, and the lemon zest and juice. Reserve a small handful each of the cilantro, onions, and pine nuts; mix the rest into the couscous. Season with more salt, pepper, and oil if desired. Transfer to a nice serving bowl and scatter the reserved ingredients on top, along with another drizzle of oil.

For my money, there's nothing better than a cup of builder's tea around 4 pm.

Inspired by British builders, who refused to work a home without a kettle, the afternoon tea break is also a hallowed time of day for carpenters, painters, electricians, and decorators on the job. For entertaining, I always love a proper teatime, with pretty bone china cups and saucers served alongside crustless cucumber tea sandwiches and assorted dainties. But when I'm working an installation, I want my tea down and dirty. Builder's tea is a no-nonsense cuppa made with plain old black tea, like PG Tips, especially the Assam variety for head-clearing, full-bodied, industrial-strength flavor. Put two tea bags in a used, cracked mug. Add boiling water. Dump in a minimum of two teaspoons of sugar and a liberal slosh of whole milk. If you can't see the bottom of the mug, it's perfect. McVitie's digestive biscuits are the classic sidekick, but sometimes I cheat with a large slab of Fig Victoria Sponge Cake, page 106.

My dear friend and neighbor Alex Vorbeck, food connoisseur, avocado grower, and tahini maker, was our hostess this teatime. Ithaka and I thought we'd drop by and surprise her with a few taste treats. Unfortunately, she was delayed, but we got to hang out and enjoy her fabulous garden.

Fig Victoria Sponge Cake

This is a version of the classic Victoria sponge cake. Using fresh figs adds an extra element to this scrumptious, well-known treat, especially if you have picked the figs yourself. —Ithaka

1 cup (200 g) self-rising flour

1 cup (200 g) fine granulated sugar, plus 1 tablespoon, divided

1 cup (200 g) softened unsalted butter, plus more for the pan

4 organic eggs, beaten

1 vanilla bean pod, scraped

1 teaspoon vanilla extract

8 ripe figs

1 cup (250 ml) heavy cream

2 tablespoons good-quality fig jam

Preheat oven to 350°F (180°C).

In a large mixing bowl, add the flour, 1 cup sugar, and butter. Mix with a hand mixer to a fine bread crumb–like consistency. Add the eggs, vanilla beans, and vanilla extract; mix until a smooth cake batter forms.

Line an 8-inch cake pan with parchment paper and thickly grease it with a layer of butter; then sprinkle with 1 tablespoon granulated sugar. Pour the batter into the pan and place in the oven for up to 30 to 40 minutes, or until golden and firm; test for doneness with a toothpick. Remove cake from the oven and let cool completely.

Whip the cream until thick and fluffy. Wash and cut the figs into thin slices.

When the cake is cool, remove it from the pan and slice it evenly across the middle. Separate the two layers. Spread the jam evenly on the bottom layer of the cake, add a layer of figs over the jam, and gently place the top of the cake on the bottom layer. Spread the whipped cream evenly over the top. Finish by decorating it with the remaining fig slices. Serve with Earl Grey tea and any leftover whipped cream.

Cinnamon Apple Tart

This is a very rustic apple tart, not fancy or fiddly. It's very rewarding when you get to pick and forage from your own garden and see the apples used in a lovely homemade tart. This one is a favorite of Kathryn's retreater Penelope Marshall. —Ithaka

1 Sweet Short Crust Pastry (page 219, or store-bought)
6 Gala or other sweet apples, cored, peeled, and cut into thin half-moons
3/4 cup (75 g) fine granulated sugar, plus extra for sprinkling
1 rounded teaspoon ground cinnamon
1/2 cup (1 stick/100 g) unsalted butter
Juice of 1/2 lemon
Pinch of salt
2 tablespoons water
Whipped cream or crème fraîche, for serving

Preheat oven to 375°F (190°C).

Fit your rolled-out pastry dough into an 11-inch (28 cm) tart pan (loose bottom works best). Blind bake the pastry for 15 to 20 minutes; the pastry should turn a nice golden color. (I like the pastry to be quite crunchy, so I tend to leave it in a little longer.) While the pastry is blind baking, start on the filling.

Place the apples, 3/4 cup sugar, cinnamon, butter, lemon juice, salt, and water in a pot over low to medium heat and let simmer for 5 to 7 minutes. You want a sort of caramel-like sauce to coat the apples; stir occasionally to prevent burning; do not overcook. Remove from the heat and let cool in the pan.

Remove the tart shell from the oven and reduce the temperature to 350°F (180°C). For a pretty tart, begin filling the shell with the apples, starting in the middle, making a concentric circle with 3 apple slices; then follow those around with the rest, layering as you go. Once the shell is filled, pour any leftover sauce from the pan over the apples and sprinkle the tart with a pinch of sugar. Bake for 25 minutes, or until golden and cooked. Remove from the oven and let cool for 10 minutes before removing the tart from the pan. Serve warm with whipped cream or crème fraîche.

BALSAMIC ROASTED STRAWBERRIES

Just recently, I discovered a new way to consume the non-stop profusion of strawberries that comes with summer. These roasted strawberries deliver a sophisticated taste profile that is surprisingly versatile. The trick is to roast them in good balsamic vinegar. Here's how to do it:

Preheat oven to 350°F (180°C). Cut 1 pound of strawberries in half and place on a parchment-lined baking sheet. Sprinkle with 2 tablespoons sugar, splash with 4 tablespoons balsamic vinegar, 1 teaspoon vanilla, and sprinkle with a pinch of salt and pepper. Mix gently, being careful not to bruise the berries, then spread out. Roast for about 30 minutes, stirring halfway through, until vinegar is reduced to a syrup. Roasting the berries deepens their flavor, rendering them jammy and robust. They enhance everything they touch: toast, yogurt, ice cream, oatmeal, grilled meat, goat cheese—the possibilities are endless. —Kathryn

Eton Mess

A classic, old-school English dessert, Eton Mess is the guiltiest of pleasures. After you macerate fresh chopped strawberries in sugar, whip your cream, and crumble a packet of store-bought meringues, you're one step from the finish line. Just smoosh it all together and voila! An easy, fast, no-bake dessert that looks positively elegant spooned into beautiful glasses. (If you want to be highbrow about it, you can make your own meringues.) It's one of my staples and the boys' favorite.
—Kathryn

SERVES 16

4 pints fresh mixed berries
(raspberries, strawberries, blackberries, redcurrants)
Sugar, if needed
4 large meringues (purchased or homemade), crushed (about 2 cups)
2 cups whipping cream
2 cups crème fraîche

Mash the berries so they form their own sauce. Add sugar to taste. Whip the cream until stiff peaks form, then fold in the crème fraîche. With clean hands, crush and mix together the meringues, cream mixture, and berries. Refrigerate for at least a couple of hours. Serve chilled.

Fresh and Easy Mint Chocolate Ice Cream

The reason this is so easy is that it's a bit of a cheat. But the fresh mint and the dark chocolate chips give it such a fresh and delicious homemade taste. —Ithaka

SERVES 6

1 pint (500 ml) good-quality vanilla bean ice cream
1 bunch fresh mint leaves (about 30 leaves)
1 cup (150 g) dark chocolate (I like Green and Black's)

To start, make sure your ice cream has been at room temperature for at least 10 minutes so that it's a bit soft and creamy. Transfer it to a large bowl.

Wash and finely chop the mint, then roughly chop the chocolate into small chips. Using a spatula, fold the mint and chocolate into the ice cream bowl, giving it a good stir so that it is evenly flavored. Return to the freezer and serve for dessert when ready.

DESSERT WITHOUT REGRET

Sugary confections are my weakness. Raising three boys, my kitchen was deluged with all manner of ice cream, cakes, and doughnuts. There was never enough kale in my garden to offset my intake of sweets, or enough pleasure from every luscious sugary bite to wipe out the regret of indulgence. But when I started summering in France, I was always struck by how guiltlessly the French enjoyed their patisserie sweets and how little obesity was on display. Then I noticed that moderation plays a key role in the eating behaviors of the French, and dessert portions are just large enough to deliver a sweet stroke to the end of a meal. The French don't snack; in fact, it's frowned upon. They don't gorge. And they don't buy processed treats; they bake from scratch using simple, quality ingredients. *Vive les desserts!*

Flourless Hazelnut Chocolate Cake

I think I was about twelve years old when I made up the most delicious, rich chocolate cake — it was perfect. I didn't follow a recipe; I just made it up as I went along. The next day I tried to repeat it and it failed miserably. It was all good practice, though. Now I much prefer this cake made with hazelnut meal. —Ithaka

1 cup (200 g) dark cooking chocolate
1 cup (200 g) unsalted butter
6 eggs, separated
1 cup (200 g) fine granulated sugar
2 1/4 cups (250 g) ground hazelnuts
   (hazelnut meal)
1 teaspoon baking powder
1 teaspoon vanilla extract
Pinch of salt

FOR THE TOPPING:
1/4 cup (50 g) butter
2 teaspoons sugar
Pinch of salt
2 tablespoons whole hazelnuts
Whipped cream or crème fraîche, for
   serving

Preheat oven to 400°F (200°C). Grease and lightly flour a cake pan.

Start by greasing a cake tin with butter and a very light layer of flour.

In a double boiler, melt the chocolate and butter on low heat; then set aside to cool.

Beat the egg yolks and sugar together with an electric mixer until they turn pale and creamy. Add the ground hazelnuts, baking powder, vanilla extract, and salt; mix well.

In a clean bowl, beat the egg whites until stiff peaks start to form.

Stir the chocolate and butter mixture into the main batter until well mixed. Then fold in the egg whites. Pour the batter into the prepared cake pan and bake for 35 to 40 minutes, or until firm. Test for doneness by inserting a small knife tip or toothpick in the center. When cooked, remove cake from the oven and let cool for about 20 minutes.

For the topping, melt the butter with the sugar, salt, and hazelnuts until a caramel starts to form and the nuts become golden and toasted. When cooled, roughly chop the nuts and sprinkle over the cake. Serve with whipped cream or crème fraîche.

Meringue M'Lord's Crystallized Violet Meringues

This recipe is from my friend Matt, who makes the best meringues I have ever had. They are crunchy on the outside and soft and gooey on the inside.
—Ithaka

- 6 medium-sized eggs, separated
- About 1 pound (500 g) fine granulated sugar
- Violet baking flavor*
- 1/4 cup (50 g) crystallized violets*
- Violet gel paste food coloring*

PIPING BAGS AND GREASEPROOF PAPER ALSO NEEDED.

*NOTE: MOST SPECIALIZED BAKING SHOPS WILL HAVE THESE VIOLET PRODUCTS.

FOR THE MIXTURE

Preheat the oven to 400°F (200°C). Line a deep metal baking pan with greaseproof paper.

Weigh a large bowl, then separate the eggs, putting the whites in the bowl; keep the yolks separate. Weigh the bowl of egg whites to calculate how much the whites weigh. Weigh out twice the amount of sugar as egg whites and place the sugar in the lined baking pan. Place the sugar in the oven for around 10 minutes. Check occasionally to see if it has started to turn brown on top and around the sides of the pan. When the sugar has a golden crust, it is ready to come out of the oven. Turn the heat down to 210 to 225°F (100°C); leave the door open to cool the oven as quickly as possible.

Using an electric mixer, beat the egg whites on low speed for about 3 minutes. When bubbles start to form, increase to medium speed. Continue beating until very stiff peaks form and you can hold the bowl upside down. With a large spoon, start adding the hot sugar to the egg white mixture while continuing to beat on medium speed. Once all of the sugar has been added, set the mixer to high speed.

After 10 minutes, the egg white mixture should become very thick and shiny, with a glossy sheen. Stop mixing and dip your finger into the meringue; a small peak on the end of your finger should form without it flopping down. Add about 5 drops of the violet flavoring and fold into the mix.

FOR THE PIPING

Depending on the size of your meringues cut the end of the piping bag off so it leaves a hole around 1/2 to 3/4 inch (15 to 20 mm) in diameter.

Turn the piping bag inside out. With a brush, paint 3 to 4 stripes of violet food gel and work down the bag from the tip to the base. Turn the piping bag back the right way and add the egg whites. Pipe the mixture onto the paper-lined baking tray to form little meringue-shaped kisses. Leave about 1 inch of space between them. Crunch up the crystallized violets and sprinkle some on top of each meringue.

Bake at about 210°F (100°C) for about 40 to 60 minutes, or until the bottoms of the meringues start to harden. Once cooked, remove from the oven and leave them to cool. Serve with blackberries and fresh whipped cream.

Al Fresco

Summer is for brights

When the weather is glorious, there's nothing better than a picnic in a lovely al fresco setting. Sitting on the ground en plein air somehow makes food taste even more delicious. Whether picnicking at the beach, on a boat, or in the middle of a meadow, I personally prefer casual foods that require minimal utensils. But you can take anything anywhere as long as you pack properly and conscientiously. Here are a few tips I've picked up through the years. Use resealable glass containers as much as possible, because food always tastes better in glass. Keep everything cold in your basket with refreezable ice packs; or freeze water bottles, which you can later drink as they defrost; or fill resealable bags with ice cubes for an ad hoc ice pack. They'll chill food during transport and you can add them to drinks at the picnic.

Make sure that cooked food has cooled completely before packing, because it can spoil and harbor bacteria if not kept at the right temperature. In fact, don't eat anything that has been left out in warm weather for more than two hours. I don't care how good it looks.

Grilled Shrimp Skewers with a Cherry Tomato and Pernod Salsa

This is a version of a recipe my father makes in the summer. It's fresh but has a kick to it; the flavors of the Pernod, tomatoes, and fresh parsley complement each other very well. —Ithaka

SERVES 6

6 bamboo skewers
24 medium shrimp (about 2 pounds/ 900 g), shelled and deveined, tails on
4 tablespoons (50 g) unsalted butter
Extra virgin olive oil
5 green onions, finely chopped
3 garlic cloves, crushed, divided
1 large pinch of vegetable bouillon powder (I like Marigold)
3 1/2 cups (500 g) cherry tomatoes, washed and halved
1 teaspoon chili powder
1 teaspoon sugar
4 mint leaves, finely torn
2 tablespoons Pernod
1 squeeze of lemon juice
Sea salt
Ground black pepper
1 large bunch flat-leaf parsley, roughly chopped

Soak the skewers in warm water for at least 20 minutes. If you can get shrimp that are shelled and cleaned, your prep time will be shorter; otherwise, begin by peeling and cleaning them. Skewer 4 of them per stick and set aside.

In a large frying pan over medium heat, melt the butter with a drizzle of olive oil. When it's sizzling, add the onions, 2 cloves of the garlic, and bouillon; cook for about 1 minute. Then add the tomatoes, chili powder, sugar, mint leaves, and Pernod. Let simmer for up to 10 minutes, until the tomatoes become soft and start to break. Turn down the heat.

In a grill pan over medium heat, add a drizzle of olive oil. When the pan becomes hot, add the remaining garlic and the shrimp skewers along with the lemon juice and a pinch of salt. When the shrimp turn coral pink, they are ready. It only takes a few minutes, so make sure not to overcook them. Transfer the shrimp from the skewers into the pan of tomatoes and toss together. Season with salt and pepper, then transfer to a serving dish and scatter the parsley.

Fresh Watermelon and Mint

This is not so much a recipe as a combining of two wonderful ingredients: watermelon and mint. —Ithaka

You will need 1 seedless watermelon and a bunch of fresh mint leaves, roughly chopped. Cut the melon into pizza slices and sprinkle with mint. It's one of the freshest combinations you will try and is great for a picnic.

NOTE: ON THE FACING PAGE IS WATERMELON JUICE. WHIR IT UP IN YOUR BLENDER FOR A MOST REFRESHING LIBATION!

Picnic-Friendly Menu Ideas

- Mason jar caprese
- Quiche
- Sandwiches, wraps, and stuffed pita pockets
- Pasta salad
- Hard-boiled or deviled eggs
- Olives
- Baguettes
- Charcuterie
- Roasted or fried chicken
- Watermelon or any fresh fruit
- Cookies or cupcakes
- A Provençal rosé; or cold beer mixed with lemonade for a shandy
- Kid-friendly drinks — lots of juice, lemonade, and water
- Espresso in a thermos

GEAR FOR A RELAXING, HASSLE-FREE, PERFECT PICNIC

- A large basket and/or cooler
- An oilcloth tablecloth
- Blankets and throws
- Moroccan floor pillows
- Umbrella
- Enamel or melamine plates and cups
- Acrylic stemless wine glasses
- Cloth napkins
- Sea salt and pepper grinder
- Condiments in mini jars
- Folding knife
- Small cutting board
- Bottle opener/corkscrew
- Citronella candles
- Organic bug spray
- Sunscreen
- Games — croquet set, paddle boards, backgammon
- A good book or magazine
- Hand wipes
- Trash bags

Mixed Vegetables on the Grill with Salsa Verde

Select any fresh vegetables and herbs that you like; below are some of my favorites. A great outdoor space and a working barbecue grill are the makings for a casual and easy Sunday afternoon lunch, when you have lots of friends and kids to cook for. The smokiness of the grilled vegetables mixed with the oil and rosemary creates delicious flavors. Fresh salsa verde kicks it up a notch and also works well with grilled fish or meat. —Ithaka

2 red bell peppers, seeded and cut into wide slices
2 yellow bell peppers, seeded and cut into wide slices
2 eggplants, sliced into circles
2 green zucchini, sliced thinly lengthwise
2 yellow straight-neck squash, sliced thinly lengthwise
3 baby cauliflowers, cut into quarters
1 large white onion, peeled and cut into wedges
Extra virgin olive oil
Sea salt
1 garlic clove, crushed
1 sprig rosemary, leaves finely chopped

SALSA VERDE
1 bunch parsley
1 bunch basil
1 bunch mint
A handful of arugula (rocket)
1 garlic clove, peeled and sliced
1/2 teaspoon sugar
2 teaspoons white wine vinegar
Juice of 1/2 lemon
Sea salt
Freshly ground black pepper
Extra virgin olive oil

Prepare your charcoal grill and burn off the coal to get it to the right temperature for cooking. (If you have a gas grill, then you don't need as much time to set up.)

Once your vegetables are sliced and ready, put them into a large mixing bowl; drizzle with a generous amount of olive oil, a pinch of salt, the crushed garlic, and the chopped rosemary. Toss together so they are lightly coated; let marinate for 10 minutes or so while you make the salsa verde.

For the salsa verde: In a blender or food processor, add all the herbs and arugula along with garlic, sugar, vinegar, lemon juice, salt and pepper to taste, and a large splash of olive oil. Blend on medium speed until the mixture becomes a salsa consistency, almost liquid. Taste and adjust seasonings as desired; add more olive oil or vinegar if the mixture is too thick. (I sometimes add a teaspoon of water to loosen it.) Then transfer salsa to a bowl and set aside.

For grilling: You will need long tongs and a platter. Arrange vegetables on the grill, monitoring the temperature to prevent burning. Grill the vegetables until they are tender and charred all over but not charcoaled, 10 to 12 minutes. Transfer to a platter and serve. Pass Salsa Verde in the bowl.

Watching Kathryn prepare for any meal, inside
or out, is like a real performance. She's like
a whirling dervish, spinning around transforming
any space in her signature style, preparing
delightful, delicious dishes from whatever pops
up in her garden. Cooking and entertaining is the
way she celebrates *la joie de vivre!*

—Carolyn Englefield, Interiors Editor, *Veranda*

You can make summer
last longer with high-
performing outdoor
fabrics. Not only do
they hold up to burning
sun, pouring rain,
accidental spills, wet
hair, sandy bathing
suits, and muddy paw
prints, but they also
deliver a graphic
dose of pattern and
bold color to outdoor
entertainment areas.

For my outdoor dining area in Santa Monica, the disheveled, rustic elegance of natural textures, Spanish influences, and earthy-hued accents creates a warm and inviting ambience for year-round entertaining.

Lulu's Herb Marinated Lamb Chops

A delicious recipe for outdoor grilling from *The Entertainologist*, Lulu Powers.

SERVES 6

MARINADE:

- 1 cup fresh mint leaves
- 1/2 cup fresh parsley leaves
- 1/2 cup fresh rosemary leaves
- 1/2 cup freshly squeezed lime juice
- 5 garlic cloves
- 1/4 cup grade A or B maple syrup
- 1/2 cup extra virgin olive oil
- 1 teaspoon Tabasco
- 2 teaspoons salt
- 1/2 teaspoon freshly ground black pepper

- 2 racks lamb (about 3 pounds), cut into individual chops

Place all marinade ingredients in the bowl of a food processor and blend.

Pierce the skin of the lamb chops with a fork several times and place it in a ziplock bag. Pour three-quarters of the marinade over the lamb and marinate in the refrigerator for at least 1 hour or up to 24 hours.

Remove the lamb from the refrigerator at least 15 minutes before grilling.

Grill the lamb over medium heat for 2 to 3 minutes per side for medium rare, or until a thermometer registers 140 degrees, using the remaining marinade to baste the lamb. If you don't have a grill, use a grill pan or a broiler heated on high.

Rosemary and Mint Roulade

Recipe from *The Entertainologist,*
Lulu Powers.

SERVES 8

MERINGUE:

    8 large egg whites
    1 cup Rosemary Mint Simple Syrup
        (below)
    2 teaspoons vanilla bean paste
    2 teaspoons white wine vinegar
    2 teaspoons cornstarch

MASCARPONE WHIPPED CREAM:

    4 ounces mascarpone cheese
    1 tablespoon Rosemary Mint Simple
        Syrup
    2 cups heavy cream
    3 tablespoons malted milk
    1 tablespoon vanilla bean paste
    3 cups fresh mixed berries
    2 tablespoons julienned mint

Line the base and sides of a 9 x 13-inch pan with parchment paper, making sure to overlap all edges. Spray parchment with coconut spray.

For the meringue: Preheat oven to 350°F (180°C). In a large bowl, beat the egg whites with an electric mixer until they begin to firm up. Add the Rosemary Mint Simple Syrup to the whites in a slow stream. Continue beating until a firm, glossy peak forms. Slowly add in the vanilla, vinegar, and cornstarch. Spread the mixture inside the prepared pan and level with an offset spatula.

Bake for 25 to 30 minutes, until a crust forms and the meringue is cooked through. Remove from the oven and let cool. Unmold the cooled meringue onto a fresh piece of parchment paper. Slowly peel off the lining paper.

For the Mascarpone Whipped Cream: Place the mascarpone and Rosemary Mint Simple Syrup in a mixing bowl and slowly whisk until smooth. Then slowly add the cream and turn the mixer up for about 4 minutes, until the cream is whipped.

Spread half of the Mascarpone Whipped Cream over the meringue. Leave room around the edges. Scatter 2 cups of the berries evenly over the whipped cream.

Roll up the meringue into a log shape. Carefully transfer the log onto a serving dish. Use the remaining cream to cover log. Chill for at least 30 minutes. When ready to serve, adorn with julienned mint and sprinkle with remaining berries.

ROSEMARY MINT SIMPLE SYRUP

In a pan, heat 2 cups water, 2 cups sugar, 1 cup pulled mint, and 1/4 cup rosemary. Bring all ingredients to a boil. As soon as it coats a spoon, turn off the heat and let it cool.

Strain out the herbs and place syrup in a jar. Keep extra for a sneaky!

Fresh Juice Gin Cocktail

Recipe from *The Entertainologist*,
Lulu Powers.

MAKES 1 DRINK

> 1 ounce fresh clementine juice
> 1 ounce fresh lime juice
> 1 ounce fresh lemon juice
> 1 ounce Rosemary Mint Simple Syrup
> 4 ounces gin
> Julienned mint, for garnish

Put all ingredients in a cocktail shaker or
Ball jar with ice and shake. Pour over ice
cubes with rose petals frozen inside them
(see page 166). Add a sprinkle of julienned
mint.

WHEN ONE IS ENTERTAINING

● All you need are the
three "P"s: Prosecco,
Parmesan and Potato chips.

● You always need a good
sneeky (aka cocktail).

● There are no rules in
entertaining — you're the
boss, applesauce! Follow
your instincts, and if
you're not a party pro,
ask your friends who are.

xo,
Lulu Powers,
The Entertainologist

Roasted Cherry Tomato and Fresh Pesto Bruschetta

This is a great predinner starter or afternoon snack. It's hearty, yet the freshness of the pesto tastes so summery, especially if your basil is from the garden or farmers market. The super sweet tomatoes create a perfect balance of flavors. —Ithaka

SERVES 12

2 3/4 cups (400 g) mixed cherry
   tomatoes—yellow, red, and orange
Extra virgin olive oil
Balsamic vinegar
1 teaspoon granulated sugar
Sea salt
Freshly ground black pepper
3 sprigs rosemary
1 whole garlic bulb
Fresh Homemade Basil Pesto (page 36)
   or chiffonade of basil, for serving
1 loaf Polâine (sourdough) bread or
   small baguette

Preheat oven to 350°F (180°C).

Wash the tomatoes and cut some of them in half, leaving a few whole; place on a baking tray. Drizzle with olive oil, splash with balsamic, sprinkle with sugar, salt, and pepper. Place the sprigs of rosemary whole on top. Cut the bulb of garlic in half and place on the tray. The garlic will caramelize slightly and become very soft and delicious; the cloves will fall out easily when cooked.

Place the tray in the oven and let the vegetables roast until completely soft and falling apart. (By the way, this is the basis for a really good tomato sauce also.)

Meanwhile, prep the Fresh Homemade Basil Pesto or chiffonade a few basil leaves for garnishing.

Next, cut the bread into 1/2-inch slices and set them on another baking tray. Brush each slice with olive oil on both sides, and sprinkle with salt. Broil or grill for 5 minutes on each side, or just until they turn golden. Remove from the oven or grill and let cool a bit.

Using a peeled garlic clove, lightly rub each piece of toast. When the tomatoes are ready, remove the skin of the whole garlic and lightly mush it into the tomatoes.

Arrange your toasts on a big wooden board. Top each slice with a tablespoon of the cooked tomatoes or whatever will fit without falling off the sides. If the slices are too large to be consumed in a bite or two, cut them in halves or thirds, as they can be messy to eat. To finish, add a dollop of pesto or a few slices of basil. Serve right away, before the tomatoes make the toasts soggy.

Tomato Provençal

Our lovely friend Mia Lillingston, who is half French, often comes down in the summer months to help cook at some of Kathryn's design retreats at her country home. Here is Mia's recipe for stuffed tomatoes. When you have a big lunch to prepare, this is a really delicious and easy accompaniment to fish or meat.
—Ithaka

SERVES 6–8

2 slices day-old bread
Extra virgin olive oil
1 shallot, finely chopped
2 garlic cloves, crushed
1 teaspoon chopped thyme
2 sprigs parsley, chopped
1/2 teaspoon paprika
Sea salt
Freshly ground black pepper
3 teaspoons Dijon mustard
7 ounces (about 200 g) Gruyère cheese, grated
8 large tomatoes
Basil, for garnish

Preheat the oven to 400°F (200°C).

Toast the bread, cut off the crusts, and break into a food processor to make crumbs. Add 2 tablespoons of olive oil along with the shallot, garlic, herbs, and paprika, and pulse briefly to combine all the ingredients. Season with salt and pepper to taste. Transfer to a bowl and mix in the mustard. Mix in the cheese, reserving a handful to sprinkle on top.

To prepare the tomatoes, cut off the tops and gently scoop out the flesh. Place tomatoes on a baking sheet. Spoon in the breadcrumb mixture, filling each tomato to the top. To finish, drizzle with olive oil and sprinkle on a pinch of the cheese. Bake for about 25 to 30 minutes, or until the tomatoes are tender and the filling looks crispy and golden.

Remove from the oven and transfer to a serving dish. Garnish with a handful of torn basil.

tomato

fennel

cucumber

mint

raised beds

The Essential Kitchen Garden

Whether I am in France or L.A., the fresh garden ingredients on which I'm most reliant are herbs that I harvest by the handful. My herb garden mainstays are rosemary, thyme, lavender, parsley, sage, cilantro (the seed is coriander), chives, dill, and mint. Herbal plants are marvelously low-maintenance — just sun, water, and the routine pinching off of the flowers to encourage continuous production of leaves, because that's where all the aroma is packed. Not only do fresh herbs impart bright accents to culinary endeavors and intoxicating aroma to indoor environments, they're filled with antioxidants and essential nutrients. When you grow your own vegetables and herbs, you can use just what you need in the moment by plucking straight from the plant. Most herbs are just as pretty as shrubs or flowers, so you don't even need a formal space for growing them.

Diced Avocado Guacamole

Throughout my childhood and most of my adult life, I have spent almost every Christmas in Mexico. The way that I know how to make guacamole is not by mashing it and adding tomatoes; the guacamole I know is very simple and clean tasting. I hope you'll give it a try. —Ithaka

SERVES 4–6

3 ripe Haas avocados
4 green onions, finely chopped
1 green chili pepper, finely chopped
Extra virgin olive oil
Juice of 2 limes
1 small bunch fresh cilantro, roughly
   chopped
Sea salt
Freshly ground black pepper

"Farming avocados is the art of turning water into oil. It takes a year of sunshine and a little rain to produce a piece of fruit."

—Alex Vorbeck, avocado farm owner

Cut the avocados in half and remove the stones. Finely dice the flesh into cubes and place in a bowl. Add the finely chopped onions and chili pepper. Add a small drizzle of olive oil, the lime juice, chopped cilantro, and salt and pepper to taste. Mix gently with a spoon. Serve immediately with blue corn chips, fajitas, or Spicy Beef and Red Pepper Tacos, page 155.

AVOCADO TIPS
                —Alex Vorbeck

- For guacamole, roasting jalapeños before making the mash is a must!

- If you have too many avocados (is that possible?), you can refrigerate them to stop the ripening; use as needed.

- If you are making avocado toast, spread a layer of tahini on the toast first, then spread barely mashed avocado, finish with a squirt of lime and a sprinkle of Maldon sea salt; delicious.

Spicy Beef and Red Pepper Tacos

I made this dish with Kathryn's boys in mind. It's spicy and sweet, the perfect snack after a long football game on the beach.
—Ithaka

MAKES 6–8

- 1 white onion
- 2 red bell peppers
- 1 green bell pepper
- Extra virgin olive oil
- 1 heaping teaspoon sweet paprika
- 1 teaspoon cayenne pepper
- Sea salt
- Freshly ground black pepper
- 1 tablespoon tomato ketchup
- 2 tablespoons (25 g) butter
- 1 sprig rosemary
- 2 organic or grass-fed tenderloin beefsteaks
- 2 limes
- A handful of chopped fresh cilantro
- Soft corn taco shells
- Diced Avocado Guacamole
- Chipotle hot sauce, optional

Preheat oven to 350°F (180°C).

Cut and slice the onion into half-moons and the peppers into long strips, discarding the seeds.

In a large frying pan on medium-high heat, bring a dash of olive oil to sizzling; add the onions and cook on medium-high heat until translucent. Add the sliced peppers, spices, and salt and pepper to taste. Cook until the peppers are soft and a bit brown. Then add the ketchup.

In a separate frying pan over medium-high heat, add the butter, a pinch of sea salt, and the rosemary sprig. Fry the steaks for about 3 to 4 minutes on each side, depending how rare you like your meat.

When the steak is cooked, set it aside on a chopping board and slice it into thin strips. Add the meat to the pepper mixture, along with a squeeze of lime juice and the chopped cilantro. Combine well and fry on a high heat for a minute or so; this brings all the flavors of the meat together with the spices and peppers. Season again if needed.

While that is heating up, place the taco shells in the oven for a couple of minutes, until warm. To serve, spoon the beef and pepper mixture into the taco shells, and top with a dollop of guacamole and a squeeze of lime juice. (Add some chipotle hot sauce for more spice if you like.)

Classic Margarita

Everyone should know how to make a good Margarita. In case you don't, here is a basic guideline. —Ithaka

MAKES 1 GLASS

    2 lime wedges
    Salt for the rim of the glass
    Ice cubes
    2 ounces (50 ml) fresh lime juice
    2 ounces (50 ml) organic 123 Tequila
        Number 1 Blanco
    1 ounce (35 ml) triple sec

Rub a lime wedge around the edge of a tumbler and dip lightly in salt. Put both lime wedges into the glass.

Pour the lime juice, tequila, and triple sec into a cocktail shaker or jug with a few ice cubes. Shake or mix well. Strain and pour into the prepared glass with some additional ice cubes. Taste and try, then adjust the next one to your liking.

Rosemary and Parmesan Cornbread with Heirloom Cherry Tomato and Calendula Flower Salsa

I came up with this recipe specially for our Mexican-themed beach picnic but have since used it at dinner parties. It goes really well with the Spicy Beef and Red Pepper Tacos (page 155) and Classic Margaritas (page 156). —Ithaka

MAKES 2 LOAVES

- 1 cup (250 ml) equal parts coconut oil, olive oil, and unsalted butter
- 1 1/2 cups (250 g) polenta flour or corn meal
- 2 cups (225 g) plain flour
- 1/3 cup (75 g) granulated sugar
- Large pinch of salt
- 1 heaping teaspoon sweet paprika
- 2 teaspoons baking powder
- 3 large eggs
- 1 1/2 cups (350 ml) milk
- 1/2 cup (100 g) grated Parmesan cheese
- 2 sprigs fresh rosemary, leaves chopped
- Heirloom Cherry Tomato and Calendula Flower Salsa (page 68)

Preheat oven to 325°F (160°C). Prepare 2 loaf pans by greasing with butter and lightly flouring the inside.

In a small saucepan, melt together the oils and butter, and then set aside to cool.

In a large bowl, combine the flours, sugar, salt, paprika, and baking powder.

In another bowl, whisk the eggs and milk together, then add the slightly cooled oil mixture and continue to whisk until well mixed.

Pour the milk and egg mixture into the flour mixture, and whisk until just combined. Stir in the Parmesan and rosemary and pour into the baking pans. Bake for 55 to 60 minutes, or until golden and firm. Slice and serve with a spoon of heirloom tomato salsa.

Crudités

A platter of crudités is
the workhorse and ultimate
last-minute standby of the
appetizer genre. When you
see an assortment of sliced
raw vegetables, you expect
to taste a garden in your
mouth. Too frequently, what
you get are pre-prepped slimy
carrots, frayed celery, limp
broccolini, yellowing green
beans, and gray cauliflower.
Literally, if you're going to
use questionable vegetables,
skip it. Because half-assed
crudités are actually worse
than nothing at all. On the
other hand, if your vegetables
are fresh and snappish, and
you've made or invested in a
great dip, like a hummus or
tapenade, crudités are not
only vibrant and colorful
but healthy and delicious.
Prepping them is the perfect
chore to delegate to a guest;
if someone's hovering in your
kitchen, hand them a knife.
When the chopping ends,
arrange vegetables artfully
on a wooden board with decades
of patina. Or not. Just make
sure you don't let the dairy
dips brulée under the sun.

Dusk is the magic hour of evening, beautiful and inscrutable. It inspires me to savor its fleeting allure with cocktails and hors d'oeuvres in the cool shade of a bright green garden. It's the time guests start gathering for dinner at La Castellane, and share their adventures of the day. I like to set up a couple of small tables outside with boards of charcuterie and cheeses, a small bowl of olives and cornichons, along with baskets of crisp crostini, chilled wine, and sparkling water. Nothing heavy, nothing too involved. Just enough edible fuel to spark conversation and tame eager appetites until dinner is served.

Making Pretty Flower Ice Cubes

You will need:
• Silicone ice cube trays
• Distilled water
• Edible flowers, not too big (pansy, nasturtium, calendula, rose, carnation, violet, johnny-jump-up, impatien, hibiscus, marigold; check the Internet for other varieties)

1. Boil the water and let it cool.

2. Fill each section of the tray 1/3 with water. Place an edible flower or petals upside down in the water. Freeze. Remove tray and fill the sections to about 2/3 full with water; freeze. Remove once again and fill clear to the top with water, and freeze.

3. When you're ready to use them, they will come out of the silicone tray easily, without breaking.

4. Place them in a glass and pour in your cold liquid. Voila!

Homemade Lemonade

Everyone should make their own lemonade in the summer, especially if you can pick the lemons from a tree in your yard. —Ithaka

MAKES ABOUT 1 1/2 QUARTS

    Juice and peel of 5 unwaxed lemons
    3/4 cup (140 g) sugar
    1 cup (240 ml) boiling water
    1 quart (1 liter) water
    Ice

Using a vegetable peeler, peel off a few slivers of the rind and place in a jug. Add the sugar, lemon juice, and boiling water; give it a good stir. After the sugar is dissolved, add the cold water along with some ice, and let cool in the fridge for 15 minutes. Serve in chilled tumblers.

> Homemade lemonade is one of my favorite summertime rituals. It's always worth the effort. And once you've mastered the basic recipe, you can glam it up with subtle floral infusions and syrups.
>
> A good gin and tonic is already refreshing, but the addition of cucumber and mint elevates it to clean, summery perfection.

Cucumber Gin and Tonic

A good gin and tonic is already refreshing, but the addition of cucumber and mint gives it a fresh, summery element. —Ithaka

SERVES 1

    1 cucumber, washed
    2 ounces (60 ml) gin of choice, Gordon's or Sipsmith
    Ice
    5 ounces (150 ml) tonic water
    Juice of 1/2 lime
    Sprig of mint

Using a vegetable peeler, peel long, thin slices of cucumber and wind them carefully around the inside of a glass. Add in the gin and ice cubes, and top with tonic water, a squeeze of lime, and a few mint leaves. Serve ice cold.

Impromptu Parties

There are two kinds of parties: special occasion, which you plan right down to the last demitasse cup, and the those that take off without any real planning at all. The second kind might be my favorite, where I invite a few friends, then they invite a friend, and then this one knows that one, and the next thing you know, there are twenty people in your house and more on the way.

When this happens, just throw out the rulebook and realize that you're not so much a hostess as a facilitator. And since there are no advance expectations, there's absolutely no pressure.

I've learned to keep a "party kit" ready at all times — a small fridge tucked under a patio sideboard filled with beer and what I call "table-y" wine, blue tortilla chips, and my avocado tree. When the rudiments run out, for a small bribe I can usually get one of my sons to run out for pizza or sushi. Over the years, I've found that friends and sudden guests really appreciate the kind of permissiveness that allows for a spur-of-the-moment party on your premises.

How to Make an Ice Bowl

Here's a way to make your table sparkle! Create ice bowls decorated with flowers, herbs, or citrus slices.

You will need 2 glass or stainless steel bowls that are 1/2 inch to 1 inch different in size.

Scatter some adornments in the large bowl and place the small bowl inside; tape rims so they stay flush. Pour water in the gap between the bowls to 1/2 inch from the top. Add more adornments; arrange with a skewer. Freeze overnight.

When ready to use, let stand at room temperature on a dish towel until the bowls separate easily (about 10 to 20 minutes). Remove the tape. Lift the top bowl out and invert the bottom bowl to remove the ice bowl. Freeze until needed.

Looks fabulous filled with ice cream or sorbets, scattered with fresh berries to create a showstopper for your guests! It doesn't cost anything either—just water and flowers from the garden!

Backyard entertaining is a good excuse to go nuclear with pillows.

—Kathryn

Bring On
the Guests

When I was growing up, my family spent our holidays at a fisherman's cottage on a beach in Scotland. It wasn't a glamorous or particularly exciting destination, but it was the invitation most coveted by my brothers' friends and mine. The reason had everything to do with our parents.

I remember my mother at her Aga range, stirring a large pot of Bolognese for a cottage full of houseguests. She had a way of making everyone feel comfortable and, most of all, wanted. She allowed a wide margin of error and communicated that anything could be fixed. If a piece of stemware got knocked off the table and broke, it was never the end of the world. Watching her tend to a playmate or console a homesick friend, I realized early on that I didn't have the sole rights to her attention; my mother lived and breathed to share. All of this made a big impression on my little soul and laid the foundation for my future as a mother-of-three, Bolognese-stirring houseguest junkie. I have extra rooms in two homes on two continents and, taking after my mother, my motto is "Fill 'em up!"

Conventional wisdom says that fish and visitors stink after three days. But having your comfort zone jostled can be rewarding. A semi-regular stream of fresh faces takes the pressure off the nuclear family and promotes serendipity. The reason European children mature faster than their American counterparts is, I believe, because they've had more experiences in the home with a mixed bag of adults. All parents try to set a good example in front of children, but some unedited behavior can be useful, either as a cautionary tale or just for a laugh. The trick is not to think of houseguests as crimping your style. If you embrace the idea that you can't have raucous sex, go to the bathroom with the door open, or eat dinner over the sink, then you're up for the challenge of taking in a few stragglers.

I have what I call a barracks mentality, so I don't think in terms of individuals; my baseline of measurement is the platoon. When I saw my property in France for the first time, I didn't covet it for my own pleasure; I saw it as a place where my kids could bring their friends and my friends could bring their kids and we could all share an unpretentious country way of living.

I keep my guest rooms as simple as possible. To me, the successful room functions like a hotel suite — clean and neutral, with good mattresses, good pillows, and empty closets and dresser drawers. I always have more blankets than are necessary. I don't mind frayed towels, but I can't stand dingy or stained ones. I like to place a couple of books by the bed, but this isn't essential. I do insist, however, on quality reading lamps.

Like my mother, I'm an easygoing hostess. All I require is that everyone embrace the communal environment. I like doers who are generous with their time. I love it when someone offers to cook lunch for the group or organizes a predinner soccer game. Those who pitch in and are hands-on, whether tending the kitchen garden or feeding the horses, are always invited back. Everyone is free to do whatever he or she wants all day, but sharing a big meal at night is de rigueur. It's a time when kids are encouraged to talk and interact with adults. It's all about communication, friendship, and eye contact. Lose the phones.

Everyone knows I'm not an heiress; I work hard for my money. And when my accountant tells me at the end of the year how much my summer cost me, it's always a shock. But the reason I work hard is so I can splurge on houseguests for three hot, wonderfully long months and create beautiful memories for the people I love.

COAT HOOK STORAGE

In a guest room, especially a small one, a wall-mounted hook rack can provide extra hanging options. Suitable for jewelry, ties, shopping bags, bath towels, and much more, hooks are an efficient way to keep essentials at your guest's fingertips.

Grown-Up Sleepovers

I love the occasional sleepover with a good friend. The pressure of limited time is lifted; you don't have to condense conversation, confidences, and closeness into one dinner. You also don't have to call the next day and go over everything — you're both right there and can do it over breakfast. It's a relaxed, leisurely way to recharge fondness and friendship. Whether sleepovers are planned or spur of the moment, this checklist of tips will help ensure that your guest accommodation resembles the graciousness of your offer, and that your friend feels welcome and highly valued.

• Whether you have an extra room designated for guests or you're converting a sofa into a bed for the night, make sure you always have clean sheets, extra pillows, and fresh towels on hand.

• Have an array of quilts and throws for the end of the bed, according to the season.

• Add a personal touch — a note, a homemade lavender sachet, a sprig of rosemary, or a small spray of garden flowers on the pillow.

• Make sure the light bulbs are working. Dimmer switches make it more intimate for the guest.

• Set tissues and fresh water and a glass on the bedside table.

• Devote a universal charger to your guest space so your friends can keep plugged in.

• Provide a spare toothbrush and other toiletries.

Kathryn's Favorites

Tomato Pasta Sauce

This really is such a good fallback tomato sauce, as it has just a few ingredients. Once you have the base, you can add black olives, chili, or fresh basil, or turn it into a puttanesca sauce. Really, whatever you have in your pantry you could add in. —Kathryn

MAKES ABOUT 5 CUPS

6 large beef tomatoes
4 garlic cloves, crushed
Extra virgin olive oil
Sea salt
Freshly ground black pepper
1 bunch fresh basil

Start by placing the tomatoes either in a large pot of boiling water and leave for up to 10 minutes. Remove and transfer into a bowl of cold water and begin by gently peeling off the skin; it should peel off pretty easily. Roughly chop into large chunks, leaving behind the core. In a large frying pan, add a drizzle of olive oil, and when it's lightly sizzling on a medium heat, throw in the tomatoes and crushed garlic with a pinch of salt.

Let simmer on a medium heat for up to 30 minutes, breaking the tomatoes up with a wooden spoon as they cook. The tomatoes and garlic should completely disintegrate into a delicious sauce. Season again with salt and pepper, and serve with a pasta of your choice and a large bunch of fresh torn-up basil.

Chicken and Leek Pie

This is a great dish every one loves — it is very heart-warming and delicious; I am feeling hungry just thinking about it! — Mary Jane Russell (Kathryn's sister)

SERVES 6–8

    1 (4 1/2-pound/2 kg) chicken, cut into portions on the bone
    2 cups (600 ml) homemade chicken stock
    7 ounces (200 ml) white wine
    2 large sprigs thyme or tarragon
    Salt and pepper
    2 tablespoons (1 oz) butter
    4 leeks (12 oz/350 g when sliced)
    1 tablespoon water
    1 tablespoon flour
    1 1/2 cups (12 oz) heavy cream
    2 teaspoons chopped fresh thyme or 1 teaspoon chopped tarragon
    1 teaspoon Dijon mustard
    1 pound (450 g) good-quality puff pastry
    1 egg, beaten

Preheat the oven to 450°F (230ªC). Prepare a 12-inch (30 cm) oval pie dish.

Place the chicken portions in a large ovenproof casserole with the stock, wine, sprigs of herbs, and a pinch of salt and pepper. Bring to the boil then reduce heat and simmer for approximately 25 to 30 minutes, or until chicken is completely cooked.

While the chicken is boiling, melt the butter in another saucepan. Add the sliced leeks and water. Season with salt and pepper, cover, and cook gently until leeks have softened. Once cooked, remove from the pan with a slotted spoon and set aside.

Add the flour to the butter juices and stir over medium heat for 1 minute to make a roux.

When the chicken is cooked, remove the portions and set aside. Bring the chicken juices to the boil and add the cream; boil uncovered for about 5 minutes, or until the mixture has intensified in flavor; then whisk in the roux. Add the herbs and mustard. Once the chicken has cooled enough to handle, pull the meat off the bones and cut into pieces; add meat to the sauce with the leeks. Season with salt and pepper to taste.

Place the chicken and leek pie filling into the pie dish so it is full. Cover with the pastry and brush with the beaten egg. Cook in the oven for 10 minutes, and then reduce the temperature to 400°F (200°C) and cook for 20 to 25 minutes more, or until the pastry is golden brown and the mixture is bubbling.

Kathryn throws the greatest parties in her eponymous "Kathryn" style. Great eats, great drinks, great people.

— Michael McCarty

Kathryn's Cosmopolitan

If the guests are coming and you want to serve something other than wine, making a cosmo is quick and easy.

SERVES 1

> 1 generous ounce (35 ml) vodka
> 1 scant ounce (25 ml) cranberry juice (we like unsweetened)
> 1 scant ounce (25 ml) Cointreau or Grand Marnier
> 1 squeeze of fresh lime juice
> Ice cubes
> Orange slice or peel, for garnish

Place the vodka, cranberry, Cointreau, and lime juice in a cocktail shaker with a few ice cubes and shake well. Strain into a coupe glass or small tumbler, and serve with a twist of orange peel.

Carina Cooper on Stylish Entertaining

Kathryn and I have stayed firm friends ever since we first met at a party in the English countryside when we were both fourteen. Our lives have had similar trajectories: we both spent time in New York in our late teens, followed by L.A. in our early twenties; we both married film directors; Kathryn had three sons, and I had four daughters. And we are both Francophiles.

There is a wonderful farm at the end of Kathryn's property, owned and run by a magnificent old French lady named Elise. It was where we would go to collect the milk, fresh from her cows, in the evening. Kathryn had just bought her house, and I was staying there before she had arrived. Elise asked my family to supper. Twenty-five years later, it still comes up as one of my ten best dinners.

We arrived in the farmyard, where a trestle table was set with a yellow gingham tablecloth. Chickens were running in and out from beneath the table. A cat was lying on the outside kitchen window, framed by neon pink geraniums, nonchalantly licking her paw while watching the comings and goings.

Family and friends of Elise were in attendance, and looking at the amount of knives and forks, I realized that quite a few courses had been laid on. The meal started with crescent-shaped melon from nearby Gaillac (these melons are juicy and sweet, justifying a trickle of juice running down one's chin).

This was followed with homemade pâte de campagne made from their own geese; it had an earthy, nutty taste to it, and pushed into unsalted butter on crumbly, crispy baguette caused a rush to the taste buds. We had an aperitif of Pousse Rapier, which is like a brandy cocktail, and the local expression goes, "Whoever gets to finish the bottle, a baby will appear nine months later!"

The most delicious red grape wine from the local cooperative, which I can smell and taste now, rinsed down the first course. The next course consisted of the most succulent roast chicken, gratin dauphinois, and a fresh garden green salad: all the ingredients were from the garden or farm. We went on to have the best — and I mean the best — bitter chocolate mousse with a gold-leaf square placed on the top, and more Pousse Rapier.

This was followed by chèvre from the goats that bleated under the marron glacé trees. The taste — I've never had anything like it — was of lavender, as Elise had infused the cream of the cheese with lavender. So this creamy chèvre with a hint of a lavender aroma has never left me. We finished with café and Vervain Tissane. I went on to have three more children, so I probably had the last drop of Pousse Rapier.

So that was the beginning of my culinary journey at Kathryn's in the early '90s. I have spent so many summers there, and my memories of it are definitely centered around food.

We'd get boxes of apricots from Montauban market, and a whole day would be dedicated to making about ten pots of apricot and vanilla bean jam that would travel back with us in the car to London.

We'd gather the raspberries from the kitchen garden, and I'd make roasted raspberry jam in the oven, inspired by Elizabeth David's recipe. Kathryn would make her delicious berry fruit ice cream.

The Mirabelle trees at the end of the vineyard would be covered with these plump, sweet little plums, which all the children would pile into baskets; then we'd make huge tarts.

The house was always full of guests and children, as entertaining is Kathryn's forte. There were always a smattering of Hollywood names who would be staying and be caught up in Kathryn's exuberance and escapades. Copious bottles of rosé would color the summer holidays. We really did see those days through rose-tinted sunglasses.

Memories of Kathryn's France are as dreamy as they appear to be in the pictures. My children have grown up there, and

my oldest daughter, Ithaka, who has taken many of the pictures
and done the recipes for this book, is the perfect example of
the legacy that Kathryn has given us, which is access to the
bucolic, vibrant, joyful life that she created on a hilltop in
the South of France.

In Los Angeles, Kathryn's entertaining takes on a different
quality from the South of France, but it is nevertheless her
inimitable style that infuses her hosting and brings fun
and joy to all of the proceedings, with wonderful food that
complements her great sense of style and relaxed quality.

The farmers markets that pepper L.A. at the weekends
are a welcome source of ingredients, particularly heritage
produce. Being next to the great Pacific Ocean, wonderful
soft shell crabs and other amazing seafood are available for
barbecuing in the warm evenings wrapped in the soft light of
the California sunset. Wild produce that grows and is produced
up in the canyons, such as Malibu honey, are individual and
artisan. The awareness of health in California adds to the
delectability of the ingredients of each dish. Burrata from
local buffalo herds in Northern California, married to yellow,
red, and green heirloom tomatoes,
sprinkled with purple basil and
laced with golden extra virgin
olive oil, cannot be more sublime.

I hope this book will be an
opportunity for you to share the
sunflower meadows of the French
countryside and make some of the
recipes we have all delighted
in over the years, and then take
you to the salty air and orange
blossoms of Kathryn's California,
where she entertains with equally
as much panache.

Your table awaits . . .

Wine o'Clock

Occasionally I give stays at La Castellane to charities to raise money. My great friend Alex Vorbeck asked if I would donate the house. I willingly said yes.

A week before they were all to arrive, Ithaka, who was primed to look after the group with her delicious food for a week, called to ask when I was arriving. When was I arriving? I had no plans; they got the house, not me as well! Alex and I went for a drink and she told me if I ever wanted to meet some of the great tech guys from Silicon Valley, I should go. I said if I could get a miles flight in business the next day (setting the bar high) I would. Well, I got a seat and arrived at the same time as the group of fourteen.

Ithaka and Mia were the soul of the household. I whizzed in and out, and made some of the greatest friends I have to this day. We had Twitter, Apple, everything but Tinder for a week. This group was so much fun and was an eye-opener for me. They raised the bar on the wine we drank and the food we ate. Now I am addicted to the tech world. I understand the importance of a wire frame, vesting, and ultimately "getting backed."

I treat entertaining as theatre. It's showtime.
Get a good cast together, make sure the set
takes your breath away, provide great lighting,
comfortable seats, endless wine, and ensure
the food is bountiful, simple to prepare and
beautifully presented. Don't over-think, over-fuss
or worry about convention. Throw 8-year-olds next
to 80-year-olds, try and invite at least one baby
and one friendly dog, crank the music up and just
enjoy the moment. If you are the hostess, act like
a leading lady and everyone else will follow your
lead and just have a simply fabulous time.

—Sarah Standing

Duck Breast with Orange Marmalade and Thyme

This is one of my favorite meat recipes; it's so tasty and feels very French and summery. —Ithaka

SERVES 2

- 2 boneless duck breast halves
- 1 jar good-quality thick marmalade
- Boiling water
- Juice and zest of 1 orange
- 4 sprigs fresh thyme, leaves only
- 1 garlic clove, crushed
- Sea salt
- Freshly ground black pepper
- Extra virgin olive oil

With a knife, thinly score the duck skin in a crisscross pattern. Place the breasts on a roasting tray.

Scoop the marmalade out into a bowl and stir in 2 tablespoons of boiling water to dilute it. Add the orange juice and zest, thyme leaves, and garlic. Season with a little salt and pepper, and drizzle in a bit of olive oil; mix well.

Coat the duck breasts with half the marmalade mixture and let marinate for up to 30 minutes in a cool, dry place, but not the fridge.

Preheat the oven to about 350° F (180°C). Place a skillet on the stove over medium-high heat and let it heat.

Carefully lay the duck breasts in the hot skillet skin side down, and sear for 5 to 7 minutes, until the skin becomes golden and crispy. The duck will release a lot of fat and can become quite spitty, so a splatter guard is handy. When the skin is to your liking, remove breasts from the pan and let them drain off some of the fat. Return back to the roasting tray skin side down, and cook in the oven for 7 to 10 minutes, depending on how rare you like your meat.

Meanwhile, put the rest of the marmalade mixture into a small saucepan with a little bit of water and let it reduce over low heat.

When the duck is cooked to your liking, remove it from the oven, cover with foil, and let sit for 5 minutes. It's possible that some juices will run out from the meat. Avoiding the fat, spoon out the juices and sticky marmalade remnants from the tray and add to the saucepan of orange mixture; continue to let it simmer until it is the consistency of a spoonable gravy.

To serve, thinly slice the duck breast and place it on a serving platter. Finish it by pouring the marmalade gravy over the meat.

The Apricot, Chive, Lamb's Lettuce, and Toasted Almond Salad (page 209) goes well with this dish.

Perfect Roast Chicken with Lemon, Shallots, and Rosemary

I honestly think cooking a good roast chicken is one of the easiest and most delicious ways to anyone's hungry heart. I learned this recipe from my mother. —Ithaka

SERVES 4

- 1 medium or large organic or free-range chicken
- 1 lemon, halved
- 1 large bunch rosemary
- 2 garlic cloves, each cut into 3 or 4 thin slices
- 6 shallots
- Extra virgin olive oil
- 2 large pinches sea salt

GRAVY:
- Wine white
- Redcurrant jelly
- 1 heaping teaspoon vegetable bouillon powder
- 1/2 cup water
- Freshly ground black pepper

Preheat oven to 375°F (190°C).

Place the chicken in a large roasting pan. Place the lemon halves inside the chicken and stuff in the rosemary; it might stick out a little.

Make a few small incisions into the breast and legs of the chicken and push in the garlic so that it's sitting just under the skin. Peel and halve the shallots lengthwise and place around the chicken. Generously drizzle olive oil over the chicken and shallots, and sprinkle the salt, mainly over the top of the bird. It seems like a lot of salt, but it creates a succulent, crispy skin.

Cook in the oven for 30 minutes, and then baste with the juices. Turn the oven down to 350°F (180°C). The chicken should take up to 1 hour and 20 minutes. Baste it every 30 minutes. To be sure the chicken is cooked through, insert a knife gently between the leg and breast. If the juices run clear, it's ready.

A good tip that I learned is to take the chicken out 10 minutes before it's ready, cut 3 long incisions into the legs and thighs, and baste those; return to the oven. This helps the thighs to cook and become really juicy.

When it's ready, tip the chicken slightly so the juices run into the tray. This is the base for your gravy. Remove the shallots and chicken to a board and cover with tin foil and let rest for 15 minutes.

For the gravy, place the tray on top of the stove on medium to high heat. Add a dash of white wine, a dessertspoon of redcurrant jelly, some bouillon powder, 1/2 cup of water, and pepper to taste; let simmer and reduce.

To serve, I like to carve the chicken and pour the hot gravy all over it, with the shallots on top. This way, all the meat is full of flavor and everyone has chicken soaked in juicy gravy.

French Green Beans with Garlic

Green beans simply steamed or boiled is probably the favorite vegetable we serve our guests. Grown-ups and kids alike really love these. —Ithaka

SERVES 5

2 2/3 cups (300 g) slender green beans, washed
Extra virgin olive oil
2 garlic cloves, crushed
Balsamic vinegar di Modena
1 bunch flat-leaf parsley, finely chopped
Sea salt
Freshly ground black pepper

Top and tail the green beans. Bring a pot of salted water to the boil. Blanch the beans for 2 to 3 minutes; they should be just tender and still a bit crunchy. Remove them from the heat and drain the hot water before the bright green color starts to fade. Rinse the beans in cold water to stop the cooking.

Re-use the pot. Drizzle in some olive oil and heat it. Add the garlic and cook for about 30 seconds. Add the green beans and toss until lightly heated. Add a splash of vinegar and the chopped parsley; season with salt and pepper to taste, and mix well.

Serving suggestions: The beans go well with new potatoes and a whole baked salmon.

Risotto with Asparagus, Peas, and Mint

This is an easy recipe for when you want to serve a quick and filling no-fuss supper. All you need is a green salad and hungry mouths to go with it. —Ithaka

SERVES 4–5

Extra virgin olive oil
1 large yellow onion, chopped
1 garlic clove, crushed
2 1/3 cups (500 g) arborio rice
1 tablespoon vegetable bouillon powder
1 1/5 quarts (1.5 liters) boiling water
7 ounces (200 ml) dry white wine
1/3 cup (70 g) unsalted butter
1/2 cup (100 g) frozen or fresh garden peas
1 bunch thin asparagus, tough ends removed, cut into thirds
1 cup (200 g) freshly grated Parmesan cheese, plus more for serving
Zest of 1 lemon
Sea salt
Freshly ground black pepper
1 bunch fresh mint leaves, chopped

Heat 2 tablespoons oil in a large skillet over medium heat. When the oil is shimmering, add the onion and garlic and cook until soft.

Add the rice and bouillon powder together. Stir so the powder gets absorbed, then add in half the boiling water and let simmer on medium heat, stirring almost constantly to prevent sticking to the bottom of the pan. Keep adding the rest of the water a little at a time, letting each addition be absorbed before adding more. The risotto should be al dente, like pasta, but not undercooked. The whole process should take about 15 minutes. Add more boiling water to the rice if necessary.

I like to add in the wine and the butter after 10 minutes of cooking so the flavors are still apparent. Five minutes before serving, add the frozen peas and asparagus along with half the Parmesan and the lemon zest. Season with salt and pepper to taste. The greens will cook in the heat of the rice, so there is no need to precook them.

Just before serving, stir in the mint. Serve in a large bowl. Sprinkle with Parmesan and drizzle with olive oil.

TIPS FOR THE PERFECT DINNER PARTY

- Be prepared: clear the decks in the kitchen.

- Have as much organization as possible in the kitchen, and keep the menu simple.

- Don't be too ambitious with the food if you are cooking it yourself. It is boring for the guests if the host is strung out and in a panic. If the host is happy, the guests will be too.

- For a large dinner party, a long, narrow table is best. People can chat to other guests on the opposite side of the table, so no one is left out.

- Make the table atmospheric using simple fairy lights and wildflowers.

—Mary Jane Russell

Apricot, Chive, Lamb's Lettuce, and Toasted Almond Salad

I developed this salad recipe
when we had an overabundance of
apricots. We had made enough jams
and tarts, so this was a bit of
an experiment that turned out to
be a delightful and filling salad.
—Ithaka

SERVES 6–8

15–20 ripe apricots in season
1 lemon
1 cup (150 g) whole almonds
Sea salt
2 sprigs rosemary, divided
1 large bunch fresh chives
1/2 cup (100 g) unsalted butter
Extra virgin olive oil
1 garlic clove, crushed
Ground black pepper
1 1/2 teaspoons maple syrup
1 box lamb's lettuce

Wash and quarter the apricots and place in a large mixing bowl with a squeeze of lemon on top; set aside.

In a small frying pan over medium heat, roast the almonds with a pinch of salt and a sprig of rosemary for a few minutes, until the almonds are golden brown. Keep an eye on them as they can burn very quickly. When they are done, remove from the heat and let cool. Then roughly chop.

Using scissors, finely snip the chives into the apricots. Mix in the almonds.

In a small pan over low heat, add the butter, a large drizzle of olive oil, the crushed garlic, a dash of maple syrup, and salt and pepper to taste. When the butter is melted, let the mixture cool a little, then poor it over the apricots and toss gently.

For a pretty presentation, spread the lamb's lettuce on a flat platter or bowl. Place the apricot mixture on top and then gently incorporate some of the lettuce among the fruit.

Orange and Purple Carrots with Fava Beans, Green Onions, and Honey, Lemon Zest, and Rosemary Dressing

This is one of my favorite vegetable dishes; it's a delicious accompaniment to a roast. The colors of the carrots make it very festive. —Ithaka

SERVES 6–8

7 orange heritage carrots, stems on
7 mixed purple and yellow heritage carrots, stems on
8 green onions
2 tablespoons butter, cut into small cubes
1 teaspoon vegetable bouillon
Freshly ground black pepper
A sprinkle of sugar
Extra virgin olive oil
1 1/3 cups (200 g) peeled fava beans, fresh or frozen

DRESSING:
Zest of 1 lemon
1 heaping teaspoon runny honey
Extra virgin olive oil
1 sprig rosemary, leaves removed and finely chopped
Sea salt
Freshly ground black pepper

Preheat oven to 375°F (190°C).

Wash the carrots and cut off any stringy root bits and the green stalk, leaving only 1/2 inch of the stalk at the top. Depending on the size of the carrots, cut them lengthwise straight down the middle, leaving the smaller ones whole. Place carrots on a baking tray.

Cut the stalks off the green onions so you're left with mostly the white part. I like to slice them lengthwise down the middle and place them between the carrots. Place the butter around the tray. Add the bouillon, pepper to taste, a sprinkle of sugar, and some olive oil. Bake for 15 minutes or so, until the vegetables soften but still have a crunchy bite.

Meanwhile, pod the fava beans and add to a pot of boiling water for about 2 minutes. Drain and rinse under cold water to stop the cooking and keep their color bright. Once the beans cool, peel them; this takes a little time but is worth it.

When the carrots and onions are cooked, remove them from the oven and set aside.

For the dressing, grate the lemon zest into a little cup. Add the honey, 2 tablespoons of extra virgin olive oil, and rosemary. Mix all together and add salt and pepper to taste.

To serve, place the carrots and onions in a serving dish and scatter the beans on top. Drip with dressing.

Roasted New Potatoes with Shallots and Thyme

If you are cooking a Sunday roast or a big dinner, the potatoes are something people expect. Whether they're mashed, roasted, or baked, as long as they are on the table, the feast is complete. —Ithaka

SERVES 5

2 pounds (1 k) unpeeled, washed new potatoes (purple and red ones if available)
5 shallots, cut in half lengthwise
1 bunch fresh thyme
Extra virgin olive oil
Sea salt

Preheat the oven to 375°F (190°C).

In a large clay baking pot or a roasting tray, place the potatoes, shallots, and about 8 sprigs of thyme. Drizzle generously with olive oil and sprinkle with a large pinch of salt. Toss lightly to season the potatoes evenly. Bake for 40 to 50 minutes, or until soft and golden. Halfway through the cooking time, mix the vegetables around so the onions and potatoes don't stick to the bottom of the tray. Best served hot.

Art Direct Your Party

- Soft lighting — always everywhere. No exceptions.
- Light the room with candles — whether you have ornate candelabra on a dining table or an emergency candle shoved into an empty Chianti bottle on a windowsill, everyone looks better in candlelight. Tea lights in votive holders can transform any space into a lovely locale. Buy them by the dozens.
- Glass hurricanes with pillar candles — essential for outdoor entertaining. Invest in a few sizes and mix them up.
- Dress the rooms with flowers — be creative; any vessel can be converted into a vase for flowers or greenery.
- Silver — Every table looks smarter with touches of silver.
- Cloth napkins — Collect a range of colors and patterns, as well as plain linen.
- Tablecloths — There's nothing like a fun fabric to dress a table, indoors or out. A pressed cloth looks tidy, but don't be afraid of a few wrinkles for less formal gatherings.
- Decor — Along with lighting, decor sets the mood. Think about the atmosphere you want to create for your guests.

Host or Hostess Tips

- Invitations — Send them out three weeks in advance; e-mail is perfectly acceptable.
- Guest list — Invite people you love, people you want to get to know, and people who know how to spark conversation and good times.
- Good music — Put together a play list that suits the occasion, or play your favorite custom Pandora channel.
- Well-timed food — Serving a simple menu that appears without a hassle is better than a gourmet feast that stresses out the host or hostess. Decide on a menu that can be prepared 80% ahead of time.
- Chef — On occasion, it really pays to hire a real pro to do the cooking.
- Cocktail party — With an organized bar and a few savory finger foods, throwing a cocktail party can be relatively easy and stress free. And it should only last for three to four hours.
- Barman — If your cocktail party guest list is 25 plus, spring for a bartender so you can enjoy yourself.
- Servers — College kids can use extra cash, and why not have some attractive young people at the party?
- Drinks — In addition to cocktails, wine and champagne are equally acceptable. Always provide a good selection of nonalcoholic beverages too, with coffee toward the end of the evening.

Mixed Plum, Vanilla Bean, and Almond Tart

This tart has a really nice balance of flavors. If you have made the pastry yourself and picked the plums, it feels well deserved. —Ithaka

- 1 1/2 batches (375 g) Sweet Short Crust Pastry (page 219)
- 20–25 mixed plums (Mirabelle, Victoria, Greengage, Damson, whatever), halved and de-stoned
- 1 1/3 cups (300 g) sugar, plus 1 tablespoon extra
- 1 vanilla bean pod, split
- 2 sticks plus 2 tablespoons (250 g) unsalted butter
- 3 organic eggs, beaten
- 1 1/3 cups (300 g) ground almonds
- 1 teaspoon almond extract
- 1 teaspoon vanilla extract
- Crème fraîche, for serving

Fit your pastry into an 11-inch loose-bottom tart pan. Blind bake at 375°F (190°C) for up to 15 minutes, until the crust is dry. Set on a rack to cool.

Place the plum halves in a bowl with 1 tablespoon of sugar. Scoop out the inside of the vanilla bean pod and add the beans and the pod to the plum bowl; gently mix around, then let sit while you make the almond batter.

In another bowl, beat together the butter and 1 1/3 cups sugar until creamy. Add the eggs, ground almonds, and both extracts; lightly whisk until a smooth and creamy batter takes form.

Fill your tart shell three-fourths full with the batter. Place the plums around in the batter, cut side facing up. Carefully push the plums in, but making sure that the batter doesn't spill over. It doesn't matter if the plums are touching. If there is any remaining juice from the plums, lightly spoon it over the batter. Place in the oven on 350°F (180°C) and cook for about 45 to 60 minutes, or until the almond batter is firm and golden. Remove from the oven and let cool for 20 minutes before taking it out of the tart pan. Serve with crème fraîche.

Buttery Sweet Short Crust Pastry

You can get very good pastry at the store these days, but making your own is so rewarding. Take the time, and enjoy the buttery, crusty fruit of your labor.
—Ithaka

MAKES 1 (12-INCH) TART

> 2/3 cup (130 g) unsalted butter, cut into small cubes
> 3/4 cup (100 g) powdered sugar
> Pinch of salt
> 2 cups (250 g) all-purpose flour, more for dusting
> Zest of 1/2 lemon
> 2 egg yolks
> 2 tablespoons cold milk or water

In a large mixing bowl, cream together the butter, powdered sugar, and a pinch of salt. Using both hands, rub and pulse in the flour and lemon zest until the mixture resembles course bread crumbs. Do not overwork it; you want it to be light and crumbly. (If you are making an apple tart, you could substitute a teaspoon of cinnamon for the lemon zest.)

Now add the eggs yolks and milk to the bowl and gently work and knead together to form a ball of dough. Do not overwork it. Try and be light and confident with the pastry kneading, as too much heat from your hands will melt the butter. When the dough is formed, shape it into a fat sausage-like roll and dust it with flour; then wrap it in plastic wrap and let rest in the fridge for at least 1 hour.

The next part is a little fiddly and time consuming. Take the dough from the fridge and remove the wrap. Place the dough onto a lightly floured surface. Now cut the pastry into 3/8-inch-thick (1 cm) slices. Gently press them down into the tart pan one by one, repeating and joining the slices together like a jigsaw puzzle until the whole case is formed. When you get to the top edges of the tart pan, gently push down with your thumb so that you have a slightly thicker edge. Place the tart shell in the freezer for 1 hour, or until you are ready to use it. This stops the pastry from shrinking in the oven.

Blind bake the tart shell in a 375°F (190°C) oven for 15 to 20 minutes, until golden and crispy, before filling it. Remove from the oven, let it cool, and fill with your desired filling.

FRESH FRUIT TARTS

All you need for a fresh fruit tart is a sweet dough, a light pastry cream, fresh fruit bursting with juicy flavor, and good technique. In the summer, think peaches, plums, berries, and cherries. In the winter months, switch gears to citrus, pineapple, and mango.

Photo Credits

Deborah Anderson, 6, 30–31, 118–119, 127, 171, 182–183, 185, 186, 188–189, 196–197

Tim Beddow, 14, 53, 95, 172–173, 200 MR

Robert Benson (for *Interiors California*), 100

Lucilla Caine illustrations, 22–23, 40–41, 67, 74–75, 103, 150–151, 168–169, 206–207, 215, 222

François Halard, 85

Emma Hardy (for *Travel & Leisure*), 16–17, 26–27, 62–63, 70–71, 77, 83 TR, 86–87, 220–221

Jon Hugstad (all fabrics) 12–13, 18–19, 52, 120–121, 136–137

Kathryn M. Ireland, 11, 45, 80–81, 82 top, 83 BL & BR, 111 both, 148, 194, 195 all

Manolo Langis (for *California Homes*), 2–3, 138–139, 140, 141, 143 both, 144–145, 160–161, 174–175

Kathy Marshall, 84, 180 B, 192

Kathy Marshall and Kathryn M. Ireland, 60–61, 64–65

Ithaka Roddam, 1, 20, 24, 25, 29, 34, 36, 37, 42, 44, 46, 47 TL & TR, 48 both, 49, 50–51, 55, 56–57, 58–59 flowers, 68, 69, 72, 76, 79, 82 B, 83 TL, 88, 89, 91, 92, 96–97, 99, 104 both, 106, 107, 109, 110, 112–113, 114, 117, 125, 128–129, 133, 147, 149, 153, 154, 156–157, 158, 160–161, 162 both, 163, 164, 165, 167, 185, 190, 195, 204, 208. 211, 212–213, 216, 217, 218

Ithaka Roddam and Kathryn M. Ireland, 105, 130–131

Sidonie Roddam, 131 TL

Sean Thomas, 198–199, 201

Mikkel Vang (for *Veranda*), 5, 8, 32, 33, 38–39, 47 B, 58 TL, 123, 126, 134, 135, 176, 179, 180 T, 181, 189, 200 TL, 200 TR, BL & BR

KATHRYN M. IRELAND

Website:
www.kathrynireland.com

Twitter: kathrynmireland

Instagram: kathrynmireland

Facebook:
Facebook.com/KathrynMIreland

#KathrynAtHome

Acknowledgments

I am grateful to many people for the help they have given me, specifically:

Ithaka Roddam, for her time, energy, photographs, and recipes. She was the nucleus of the book.

Lucilla Caine, for charming illustrations that always capture visually what I am trying say.

Kate Betts, for being a great friend of many years, and for coming to the French retreat and writing a hilarious piece for Travel & Leisure and then another piece for the Wall Street Journal on our Los Angeles Design Retreats. Your pros continue to make me howl with laughter!

The magazines that I have been featured in and that appear in this book: Veranda—Carolyn Englefield, with a ruthless eye for detail and a determination to not go to bed before the shot is done! Travel & Leisure—Nancy Novograd, who made this magazine into one of the greats. California Homes—Susan McFadden, who featured a story with Lulu Powers, the delightful and "sneaky" Entertainologist.

Carina Cooper, for sharing and inspiring Ithaka with her recipes. Mary Jane Russell, my sister, for sharing her favorite recipes. Jeffrey Allen Marks, Sarah Standing, Eric Buterbaugh, Michael McCarty, Alex Vorbeck, Mia Lillingston, Jaqueline Dessoubre for friendship and for sharing quotes, and talents that make my life and design retreats enjoyable. Jane Webster, for jumping in and sitting beside me when I most needed guidance. Mel Bordeaux, for working with me from the first, some six books ago.

Doug Turshen and David Huang, for the design of another of my books.

Madge Baird, for putting up with quite a few of my midlife tantrums, and Renee Bond, for her part in bringing the pages to life.

Matt Walker and the Period Media team, for organizing the shoots that helped bring this book to life and for continuing to generate media.

A huge thanks to all the extraordinary photographers whose work appears in this book: their names appear on page 223.

To all of you that will spend time with the book.

Thank you all; I am so lucky to have such a remarkable team.